REVIS

TOOL & CUTTER SHARPENING

FOR HOME MACHINISTS

HAROLD HALL

Revised and updated by **George Bulliss**,
editor of *The Home Shop Machinist* magazine

FOX CHAPEL
PUBLISHING

Parts of this book were updated for today's American reader with regard to new techniques and tools. These updates were graciously provided by George Bulliss of *The Home Shop Machinist*, *Machinist's Workshop*, and *Digital Machinist* magazines.

Copyright © 2017 by Harold Hall and Fox Chapel Publishing Company, Inc., Mount Joy, PA

First published in the United Kingdom by Special Interest Model Books
© Special Interest Model Books Ltd 2006
First published in North America in 2017 by Fox Chapel Publishing, 903 Square Street, Mount Joy, PA 17552

Cover and back cover images by Harold Hall.

ISBN 978-1-56523-912-8

Library of Congress Cataloging-in-Publication Data

Names: Hall, Harold, 1933- author.
Title: Tool & cutter sharpening for home machinists / Harold Hall.
Other titles: Tool and cutter sharpening for home machinists
Description: East Petersburg : Fox Chapel Publishing, 2017. | Includes index.
Identifiers: LCCN 2017013666 | ISBN 9781565239128 (pbk.)
Subjects: LCSH: Sharpening of tools.
Classification: LCC TJ1280 .H275 2017 | DDC 621.9--dc23
LC record available at https://lccn.loc.gov/2017013666

To learn more about the other great books from Fox Chapel Publishing, or to find a retailer near you, call toll-free 800-457-9112 or visit us at *www.FoxChapelPublishing.com*.

Printed in Singapore
First printing

CONTENTS

PREFACE

Sharpening workshop tooling almost certainly has for most workshop owners more mystic than any other workshop activity. This though need not be so and this book seeks to give a much clearer understanding of the subject. It is though true that unlike the center lathe, where that in the home workshop will very closely emulate that in the professional workshop, facilities for sharpening will almost always be very different compared to that in industry.

Small tool and cutter grinders are available which go some way to limit the differences but if ready made will be rather expensive when considering their limited use. Designs for manufacture in the home workshop, and available in kit form, will limit the expenditure but will, in most cases, be a major manufacturing task and take up more workshop time than other projects permit. On the other hand, making one as a satisfying project in its own right will often justify the time taken.

Fortunately though, most tasks, certainly the more common ones, are possible to a reasonable standard using an off hand grinder, assisted by various simple attachments. Most of these capable of being made quickly and cheaply in the workshop itself. This book seeks to make this possible and as a result ensures that the cutters in the reader's workshop are kept in good condition. Having sharp cutters available will without doubt ensure that workshop activities are carried out with the maximum amount of satisfaction.

Having largely completed this book I came across a book on precision grinding. This starts the tool and cutter grinder chapters with the following comments.

"The subject of Cutter and Tool Grinding is most complex, due not only to the great variety of cutters and tools, but also to the various methods by which they can be ground. The ultimate success of producing accurate and correctly ground cutters depends mainly on the skill and initiative of the operator, although there are certain basic principles which must be adhered to."

While this book will undoubtedly add to the methods used I feel sure that the simplicity of many of them will remove the complexity that for good reason prevails in the commercial workshop.

Harold Hall, January 2006

CHAPTER 1
SHARPENING: AN INTRODUCTION

Ask most workshop owners, especially those relatively new to the situation, what piece of equipment is used for sharpening workshop tools and I anticipate most will refer to the "off hand grinder." While many will get by, to a greater, or more likely, a lesser extent, results will be limited both in range and in

1 The limited rest on an average off hand grinder.

quality. However, the off hand grinder, despite its severe limitations, is an essential piece of equipment for basic grinding. It is, though, totally inadequate for the cutter sharpening often attempted free hand using it. The major problem is the very limited rest provided with these, **Photo 1**.

Many workshop owners, and even some in industry, will attempt to make do with such a grinder using it solely for off hand use. Typical items sharpened in this way are screwdrivers, lathe tools and drills. This is so inadequate that I am not going to attempt any detailed explanation as to this method. Having said that the off hand grinder, as supplied, should not be used for sharpening workshop tools, it can when aided by various accessories rival that of the tool and cutter grinder for many applications.

Even with a tool and cutter grinder, sharpening workshop tooling will still be an operation fraught with complications and, sometimes, using an off hand grinder with a simple accessory will actually be easier. Number one decision to be made will be the angle at the cutting edge and, like numerous charts of machine speeds giving differing advice, reference to cutter angle details will bring up a similar situation.

2 A simple grinding rest that will increase the work possible when using an off hand grinder. Details of the design for this are given in Chapter 9.

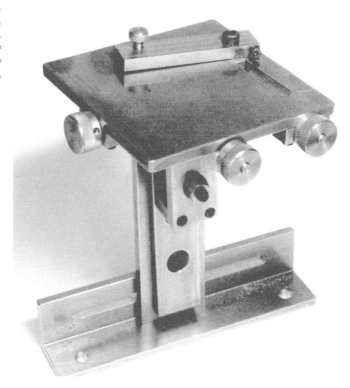

In industry, a lathe tool with a greater angle may cut easier and allow faster speeds, but the finer edge and higher speeds will result in more rapid tool wear, thereby needing it to be changed earlier in the batch. In this situation it will be a case of a balancing act between higher production speeds and longer times between tool changes. Such considerations do not occur to the same extent in the home workshop and as a result the cutter angles are not as critical. It should be obvious that a cutter with a sharp edge and not the best angle is superior to a blunt cutter but with a better angle.

The most prominent tools requiring sharpening will be drills, lathe tools and milling cutters. Where you are dealing with

tools that have been made commercially, almost always the case with milling cutters, attempt to replicate the existing angles when sharpening. A deviation of a degree or so from the original will have little consequence in the home workshop. With milling cutters therefore it is preferable to set up with reference to a cutter that has never been sharpened. More about the process later in the book.

It is probable that most workshops will be equipped with just an off hand grinder. This will suffice for most requirements, providing additional accessories are added for the purpose. The grinding rest in **Photo 2** being typical. At the other end of the spectrum, except that is for a fully equipped industrial tool and cutter grinder, is that shown in **Photo 3**. Between the two are a number of machines available in kit form for manufacture in the workshop itself.

The best known is the Quorn, (**Photo 4**) having been available for a number of years. This is a very capable machine and a very satisfying project to complete, often made to a very high standard and entered at exhibitions throughout the world. Another very adaptable machine is the Stent (**Photo 5**) following a design similar to an industrial tool and cutter grinder, but on a smaller scale. This is a quite different project in terms of its manufacture and has one facility that is not provided by the others, that is, it is capable of surface grinding.

Two simpler machines, but both capable of almost all the commonly required sharpening tasks are the Worden (**Photo 6**) and the Kennet (**Photo 7**). These appear to have

3 Vertex tool and cutter grinder.

distinct similarities in the way that they function but are constructed quite differently. The suppliers of these five grinders are given at the end of the chapter.

If, in addition to acquiring a tool and cutter sharpening facility, you would like an interesting major project then making either a Quorn or a Stent would be ideal. If, on the other hand you are looking for a means of sharpening tools without too much workshop involvement in their construction, then the Worden or the Kennet would be worth considering. The Worden being particularly easy, both in terms of time taken and the lack of complexity of the manufacturing tasks required.

The Worden and the Kennet will satisfy all common requirements, but if tools such as reamers, taps, etc., feature on your list of items to sharpen then the Quorn or the Stent would be the machines to choose. However, should you not want to spend so much time making sharpening equipment, or require a cheaper option, then some of the simple designs throughout this book will almost certainly meet most of your needs.

4 Quorn tool and cutter grinder.

5 Stent tool and cutter grinder.

will come already fitted with grinding wheels, or as part of the kit in a unit for workshop construction. No doubt having been chosen by the supplier the wheels will be adequate for most tasks undertaken on it.

There is one exception, most often the wheels supplied will suit tooling grade steels such as high speed steel but will not be adequate for grinding tungsten carbide. For this a wheel specifically for the task will be required and fitted as and when such tooling is to be ground. These are frequently known as green grit wheels and your supplier should be able to advise with more detail. An alternative to the green grit wheels would be to fit a diamond wheel. These are mainly intended for

Another possibility would be a second hand industrial machine should you have room for one.

This book seeks to achieve adequate results with the minimum of equipment. However, the Quorn and the Stent will cope with some tasks not easily carried out with the equipment described throughout this book. Because of this, if the workshop were equipped with a Quorn, a Stent, or a commercially available machine, then additional reading would be worthwhile so as to get maximum benefit from owning such a machine. In this respect, a book ("The Quorn" ISBN No. 0 905 100 91 3) detailing the construction and its use may still be found, as are books primarily intended for the industrial user.

WHEEL MATERIAL AND TYPES

Invariably, your grinder, be it a basic off hand grinder, or a versatile tool and cutter grinder,

SK1 Grinding Wheel Shapes

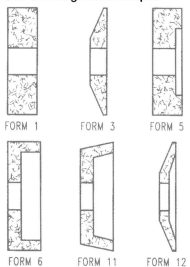

FORM 1   FORM 3   FORM 5

FORM 6   FORM 11   FORM 12

The shapes illustrated are just a few of those listed in DIN ISO 525. They are though, those most suitable for the home workshop.

use on tungsten carbide tooling but grades for high speed steel are becoming available.

Wheels come in a very wide range of shapes but most are for very specialized situations. **SK1** shows six of the more common ones that may be found useful in the home workshop. Form 1 is obviously the one that will be used on the off hand grinder with the others appropriate to a tool and cutter grinder. The fact that form 1 gives way to the other shapes when fitted to a tool and cutter grinder illustrates that these have some advantages over the simple flat disk.

In view of these advantages, adapting a bench grinder to take these wheel types, as seen in **Photo 8**, would be very worthwhile. You will though still need a grinder fitted with the normal two wheels for more basic tasks. Details for adapting a standard bench grinder to take the alternative wheels are given in Chapter 13.

With regard to the wheel material this will normally conform to the long standing types, typically an aluminum oxide abrasive with a vitrified bond.

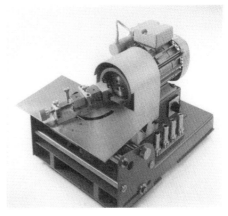

6 Worden tool and cutter grinder.

WHEEL MARKINGS

The method of marking grinding wheels is standardized and can, if purchased from a reliable source, be counted upon to provide an accurate indication of the wheel's characteristics. The marking consists of a series of numbers and letters having well-defined meanings. Prefixes and or suffixes may be added for additional data as

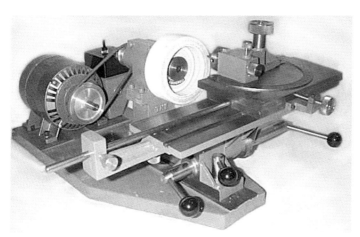

7 Kennet tool and cutter grinder.

8 Adapted off hand grinder, fitted with wheels for tool and cutter grinding. This is not intended for normal off hand use and must be used with a separate rest, typically that in Photo 2.

considered necessary by the manufacturer. The following gives the meaning of the characters that make up the marking, and are listed in the order they appear.

Abrasive. This falls into two categories, Aluminum Oxide (A) and Silicon Carbide (C). Some manufacturers have their own trade names for these and use prefixes (BA, PA, etc.) to define small variations. A Green Silicon Carbide, recommended for sharpening carbide tipped tools, is most often, though not always, marked with a G prefix (GC).

Grain size This is defined by a number consisting of one, two or three digits, the smaller the number the larger the grain size. For a general purpose off hand grinder, a coarse wheel having a grain size of 36 (0.5mm average diameter) and a fine wheel with a grain size of 60 (0.25mm average diameter) would suit most applications.

Grade. This is frequently defined as the hardness of the wheel, but should not be confused with the hardness of the abrasive; it is the strength by which the individual grains are held together and refers to the hardness

of the wheel as a whole. It is defined by a letter, with A being very soft through to Z that is very hard, though the extremes are rare. As an indication, H is considered soft, N medium and S Hard.

Structure. Best thought of as the porosity of the wheel as it defines the degree of open spaces between grains. Defined by one or two digits, 0 being dense, through to 15 being open. This characteristic is not always included in the marking.

Bond. The material that bonds the grains together is defined by this character. There are five methods, each using a single character. Individual manufactures may add additional characters to distinguish between small differences in bond method or material. The five materials are Vitrified V, Resinoid B, Rubber R, Shellac E and Silicate S. Vitrified is by far the most common. Resinoid, Rubber and Shellac enable, among other uses, thin wheels to be made for cut off machines. Silicate is for very special applications.

Typical marking. In accordance with the preceding would be BA 46 N 8 V

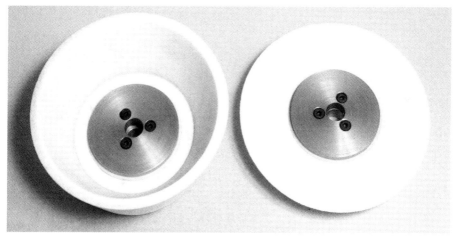

9 Tool and cutter grinder wheels with adapters.

ADDITIONAL MARKINGS

Speed. Except for smaller wheels all wheels when new are marked with the maximum speed permissible, under no circumstances must this be exceeded. The speed may be in RPM but may be quoted as the maximum surface speed, typically meters per minute.

Bore. The markings also include the wheel's bore diameter.

FITTING

Fitting a grinding wheel may seem a simple task, but it is a measure of the importance given to this, that in industry only people who have received training specifically for the task are permitted to carry it out.

It is common for wheels to have a bore larger than needed, requiring an adapter bush to be fitted. Do not use the wheel without it closely fitting the spindle on which it is used, with an adapter if required. Running a wheel with excessive clearance between bore and spindle is very dangerous. **Do not do it!** The adapter should be a close, but not

excessively tight, fit in the wheel and should not be wider than the wheel itself.

The paper disks supplied with the wheel, known as blotters, must be fitted between the wheel and the wheel flanges. The quality of the paper that these are made from is considered important but in their absence disks made from a thick, but not over hard paper should suffice. Their diameter must be greater than the flange diameter by a few millimeters to ensure that there is paper at all points round the flange.

Having assembled the flanges, blotters, wheel and clamping nut, the nut should be tightened just sufficient to reliably hold the wheel in use; over tightening may cause the wheel to fracture. This may be immediate when there will only be a failed wheel, but if only apparent when the grinder is up to speed the result may be serious injury to the user.

Wheels intended for tool and cutter grinding will have a bore much larger than the spindle onto which it is to be fitted. In this case the wheel is permanently fitted with a metal adapter that has a bore having a close fit on the grinder's spindle, **Photo 9**. This enables different wheel shapes to be interchanged without the need for balancing by dressing at each change. The blotters again must be fitted and the 3 screws tightened progressively in turn, also ensuring that they are not over tightened. Similarly, the single nut on the spindle must not be over tightened as the clamping pressure will be transferred, via the flanges, through to the wheel.

A REALISTIC APPROACH

This book seeks to take a realistic approach to the subject of sharpening workshop tooling. That is to say some items are considered practical for sharpening in the home workshop, and others not. Those not will get only a passing comment, if any. The reason for taking this course is that I believe the reduced cost of modern cutting tools makes sharpening them a non starter when the process becomes unacceptably difficult, and probably also unreliable; because of this very few workshop owners would tackle the task.

I believe reamers fall into this category with taps and dies following close behind. Another factor is that reamers and taps are relatively lightly used compared to a lathe tool or an end mill, and if used and stored with care will outlast the owner's requirements.

REFERENCES

The following are the suppliers of the tool and cutter grinders shown in Photos 3 to 7.

Quorn:

Martin Model and Pattern

www.martinmodel.com

Stent:

Blackgates Engineering

www.blackgates.co.uk

Worden:

Hemingway Kits

www.hemingwaykits.com

CHAPTER 2

DRILL SHARPENING

Of all the cutting tools, the twist drill is by far the most likely to require attention, not just in the metalworking workshop but also in other trades: builders, carpenters, DIY exponents to name but a few. Because of this there are many relatively simple devices commercially available for assisting with sharpening them, a situation that does not occur with any other cutting tool where the user is left largely to his or her own devices, apart from, of course, purchasing a tool and cutter grinder.

THE METHODS

Available accessories for the task will divide loosely into three categories. The simplest, are those intended for coupling to a pistol drill and having a very small grinding wheel, that in **Photo 1** being an example. The twist drill is placed into the device being held in a suitable adapter and then rotated by hand causing the drill to be sharpened. There are a number of different units that basically work in this way, probably with more or less success. That in the photograph works well enough

1 Pistol drill with DIY drill sharpening device.

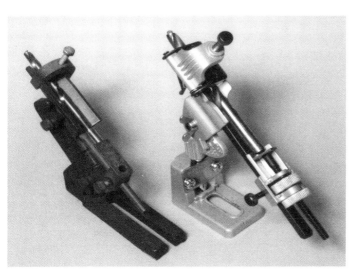

2 Reliance jig (left) and modern jig (right).

for the less demanding trades but really is inadequate for the metalworking workshop involved in precision work. Many also have a green grit wheel for sharpening masonry drills. Some that work in a comparable way are self-contained with their own motor.

The second category comprises those intended for use in conjunction with an off hand grinder. I have said "those" but at the time of writing this book, reference to around eight catalogs all show the same unit on offer. This is the one on the right of **Photo 2**. Actually, this is less expensive than those I consider DIY items.

The unit on the left of the photograph is the Reliance drill sharpening jig that was available for very many years but sadly no longer, as the modern version has some minor weaknesses compared to its older colleague. These are:

A. There is some unwanted flexibility in the pivot arrangement that is not present in the older version.

B. The drill with its immediate mounting cannot be removed from the lower part making it a little difficult to rotate the drill for sharpening the second edge.

Having said that, the modern unit is capable of good work with only a little care once one gets used to its minor limitations. It does have the advantage of the angle being adjustable for special drill shapes, countersinks, etc.

While the unit just described will also find itself in the small commercial workshop, larger organizations will most certainly have dedicated machines for the task which fall into category three. That shown in **Photo 3** is an example, capable of sharpening drills up to 13mm (½") diameter. Large companies will no doubt have an even more robust and versatile version of this. Actually, I feel that the unit in the photograph really sits between categories two and three and some home workshop owners may consider the expense of owning one justifiable.

SHARPENING DRILLS FREE HAND

There are those who will claim that they can sharpen drills free hand and no doubt some can make a very commendable attempt. However, for the majority, the limited practice one gets makes it not worth attempting, except maybe for large size drills outside the range of the available jig. There are two requirements when sharpening a drill, getting it to cut freely and getting it to cut to size. With only a little practice, getting a drill to cut freely should not present a major problem, getting it to cut to size within reasonable limits will. There is no point in having a drill set in 0.1mm increments if typically the 6.1mm drill drills at 6.3mm diameter.

It is therefore in my estimation essential to have a drill sharpening jig if the workshop is involved in precise metalworking activity. There are of course limits to the range of drill sizes a single jig can accommodate. The Reliance will work with drills from 3mm to 13mm (⅛" to ½") while the other will work up to 18mm (¹¹⁄₁₆").

As I believe that at above 18mm a larger jig would be difficult to justify, especially as this would have to be an industrial caliber item and have limited use, this would be a good situation to attempt manual grinding. Practice by holding the drill against a stationary wheel, moving the drill such that it remains in contact with the wheel from the cutting edge back to the furthest point of the clearance. Repeat the process until you feel sufficiently confident to switch on the grinder and take the first skim.

For the very small sizes the jig shown in **Photo 4** will enable smaller drills to be sharpened, at this size most probably after a drill has been broken. The jig is used on a flat stone rather than a rotating wheel. I have used it on rare occasions with some success but have never checked just how accurately the drill drilled. Details for making this jig are included in Chapter 12.

The Jigs in **Photo 2** are relatively easy to use, after a few trial runs, and give reasonable results, They are seen being used with the off-hand grinder in **Photos 5** and **6** and show

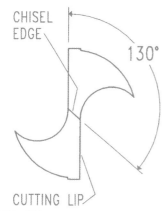

SK1. Chisel edge angle

4 Jig for very small drills, this used on a flat stone rather than a grinding wheel.

that there is a subtle difference between the two. The modern unit in **Photo 6** rotates about a spindle that is almost parallel to the grinding wheel's side while the Reliance rotates about a spindle that is at an angle of about 45 degrees to the wheel. Both units

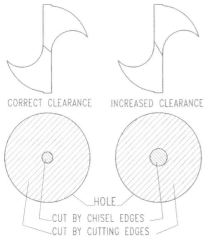

SK2. Effect of clearance angle variation on the chisel point angle and length

present the drill to the wheel at the same angle of 59 degrees but the different axis used with the Reliance causes the clearance to be created differently, more about that later. What the pros and cons of the two methods are I cannot say other than to say that both produce workable results.

As I believe the majority of workshop owners will posses the jig in **Photo 6**, or a close relative of it, I will largely limit my explanations to the method they use to produce the common drill point configuration.

Four factors make up the drill point geometry, the angle, the cutting lip length, clearance behind the cutting lip and the angle and length of the chisel point. The internal angle of the common drill is 118 degrees and using a jig will easily ensure that the angle is equal on both sides (59 degrees) so I will not discuss the effect of unequal angles. Similarly, having equal angles the lip lengths should also be the same, though this is not guaranteed unless care is taken. What can

easily vary is the clearance angle behind the cutting lip and the effect this has on the chisel point. **SK1** shows the end view of an accurately sharpened drill.

It may come as a surprise that even using the type of jig suggested, where it is quite easy to get both the cutting edge angle correct and both lengths equal, the chisel angle needs much more attention. Sketch **SK2** shows the end view of a drill with an increased chisel angle. The increased angle in the drawing shows the effect is to lengthen the chisel and shorten the cutting edges.

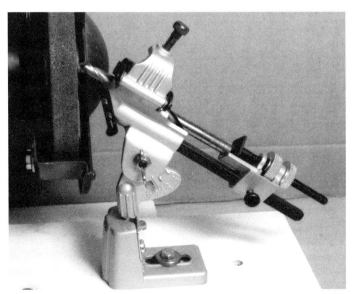

6 The modern jig in use.

7 Two drills sharpened with the wrong projection from the drilling jig. That on the left having too little projection the clearance is too great, while that on the right has too little clearance having been sharpened with too much projection.

Looking at the end of a twist drill it becomes obvious that the cutting lips are less than the radius of the hole being drilled. Because of this the chisel has to remove the center of the hole with what can only be termed a scraping action. This is the case even with a perfectly sharpened drill.

Ensuring the chisel angle is correct is therefore of considerable importance, as a longer chisel will considerably increase the pressure required to force the drill through the workpiece. Another important point to consider is that if attempting to start the hole from a center punch mark the longer chisel will find it more difficult to centralize itself on the mark.

What then causes the chisel angle to be incorrect and how can this be corrected? The cause is too much clearance angle. If the face behind the cutting lip falls too rapidly it will result in the chisel being skewed round. I think this will be better understood if you observe an actual drill, a large size preferably.

It can be seen by reference to **Photo 6**, showing a jig in position for sharpening a drill, that the jig rotates about a bearing in the base of the unit. Sketch **SK3** shows how this grinds a cylindrical surface onto the end of the drill. Of greater significance is that the radius of the cylinder will vary with the amount that the drill is projecting from the jig as the sketch illustrates. For a reduced projection the radius becomes less and the curvature greater, as a result the clearance behind the cutting edge increases. This will have the effect of increasing the chisel angle and its length.

I should add here that in the case of the Reliance, and other similar jigs, that the jig rotating about an angle to the wheel's side that the ground face is conical rather than cylindrical. However, all my comments regarding chisel angle variation and the reasons for this are equally applicable.

Photo 7 shows two drills sharpened with differing projections from the jig. The one on the left has been sharpened with too little projection and the rear clearance is far too great. On the other with more projection, the clearance is less. **Photo 8** shows how this has caused the chisel angle on the left to increase compared to that on the right. However, this photograph, set up with two old drills taken at random, has served to show another feature of drill sharpening.

THE WRONG ANGLE

It can be seen that the drill on the right has straight cutting edges, as it should have,

8 The effect of too much clearance has resulted in too great a chisel angle, while with too little clearance the chisel angle is too small. See text regarding the curved cutting edge on the left hand drill.

while those on the left have a pronounced curve. This is because, while it was sharpened at the standard angle of 118 degrees, this was the wrong angle for the type of drill that it is. While drills purchased for general use (by far the majority of the drills sold) are intended to have a point angle of 118 degrees some, for special reasons, are intended to have another angle. Typical of this are drills specially made for drilling thinner materials. These have a flatter point so that more of the drill is in contact with the workpiece before the point starts to break through. The effect of the wrong angle is that with too flat a point then the cutting edges become concave and if too pointed, convex, see **SK4**. The drill in the photograph should have been sharpened at greater than 118 degrees (flatter) and is obviously a drill intended for thin materials. For this reason, the 118 degree angle, or more or less for special drills, is relatively important but not an absolute requirement, a variation of a few degrees will not be a problem. There is therefore no need to check the angle, if the cutting edge looks straight all is well.

USING THE JIG

It would be nice to give a detailed explanation of how to use the type of jig seen in the photographs, especially as the instructions supplied often leave a lot to be desired. However, jigs purchased from different sources are likely to have differences and, similarly, also the instructions supplied. I am therefore giving the essential basics and would suggest that you arm yourself with a few old drills in the larger sizes, say 8mm to 12mm (5/16" to 1/2") and spend an hour or so attempting to put the jig through its paces.

Three things are important when positioning the drill in the jig. These are the projection, the orientation of the cutting edge and rotating the drill 180 degrees after having completed the first edge.

The earlier explanations have detailed the effect of the wrong projection from the jig but I found the instructions supplied with my jig were somewhat vague. The real important value is the distance from the jig's axis as **SK3** attempts to illustrate. This though is difficult to measure and it is normal to take a measurement off the end of the channel in which the drill rests.

However, this is not a constant and varies with the diameter of the drill being sharpened. Actually, the larger the drill the greater the required projection.

I can therefore, only suggest that initially you follow the instructions with the jig and observe the results. If this gives a chisel angle of approximately 130 degrees then all is well, if more or less then adjust the projection and re-sharpen. The angle can be checked by comparing the drill being sharpened against one of similar size that is still in the state supplied. Alternatively, a small piece of card marked at 130 degrees can be placed alongside the drill's cutting edge as a reference.

Next important requirement is the orientation of the drill, that is, does the cutting edge have to be vertical, horizontal or some angle between. For this the cutting edge should be set so that both ends arrive at the wheel at the same time, for the type of jig being considered this will be vertical. If the error is appreciable then one end of the cutting edge will arrive at the grinding wheel before the other causing the cutting edge to be domed as illustrated in **SK5**.

However, this situation is more theoretical than actual, as the error would have to be large for it to become apparent. Of more importance is that, while the cutting edge has been rotated in the jig, the chisel produced will still be produced in largely the same position relative to the jig. Rotation of the drill will therefore result in a change in the chisel angle. Orientation is, however, not critical and a few degrees either way will not cause undue errors.

Having sharpened the first side, it is very important that the drill is rotated as close to 180 degrees as is possible. Only if this is done

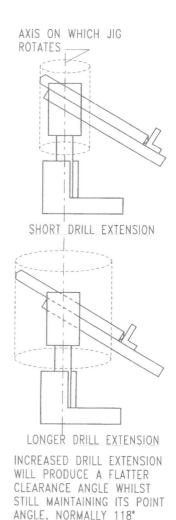

AXIS ON WHICH JIG ROTATES

SHORT DRILL EXTENSION

LONGER DRILL EXTENSION

INCREASED DRILL EXTENSION WILL PRODUCE A FLATTER CLEARANCE ANGLE WHILST STILL MAINTAINING ITS POINT ANGLE, NORMALLY 118°

SK3. Result of change in drill extension.

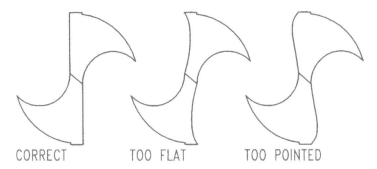

CORRECT   TOO FLAT   TOO POINTED

SK4. Effect of drill point angle variation on the cutting edge.

will the two sides be the same. The jig has a small finger that is set to locate into the flute on the first side and is then used to replicate the setting on the second. I found this difficult work with so where the drill is long enough I made a short bar to fit to the drill to control the rotation. This is best understood by studying **SK6**, and **Photos 9** and **10**.

Sharpen the first side with the drill bar against the stop bar post, then having completed that edge, rotate the drill once more ensuring that the bar is against the post and sharpen the second edge. When fastening

DOMED POINT. AS A RESULT OF NOT SETTING CUTTING EDGE CORRECTLY IN THE JIG

CORRECT DRILL POINT

SK5.

the drill bar to the drill the two halves of the bar should of course be parallel. At smaller diameters just a visual check should suffice but at larger diameters check the gap at each end with a rule.

Having sharpened your drill you can use it to drill its first hole. However, before arriving at that stage check the appearance of the drill against a new drill of similar size, in particular, the chisel angle but also the clearance behind the cutting edge. This is important for even if these are wrong the drill will probably still drill a reasonable hole. If the sharpened drill shows major differences from a new drill adjust projection and grind once more.

With the first drill sharpened correctly make a note of the drill size and the projection used. Do this with other drills, remembering that larger drills require a greater projection, until you have a range of values. From this point it will only be necessary to interpolate from these values for drill sizes that fall in between. You will soon realize that the amount of projection and the orientation of the drill are not that critical and some variation from the ideal will still give workable results. Getting close to 180 degree rotation between edges is more important.

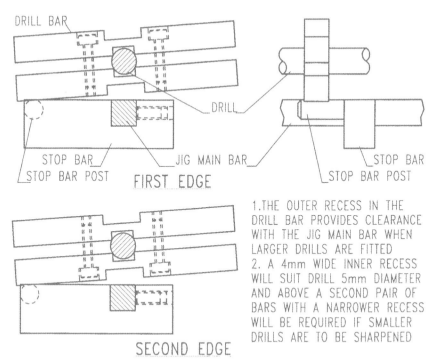

STOP BAR STOP BAR POST JIG MAIN BAR FIRST EDGE DRILL STOP BAR STOP BAR POST

DRILL BAR

SECOND EDGE

1. THE OUTER RECESS IN THE DRILL BAR PROVIDES CLEARANCE WITH THE JIG MAIN BAR WHEN LARGER DRILLS ARE FITTED
2. A 4mm WIDE INNER RECESS WILL SUIT DRILL 5mm DIAMETER AND ABOVE A SECOND PAIR OF BARS WITH A NARROWER RECESS WILL BE REQUIRED IF SMALLER DRILLS ARE TO BE SHARPENED

SK6. 180 degree rotation device.

Having set the drill in the jig with the required projection, the complete jig is moved towards the grinding wheel until the drill's edge almost touches the wheel. The slot in the jig's base permits this adjustment to be made, as can be seen in **Photo 6**. The jig then provides a fine feed to set the amount being ground off, do set this to remove very little or overheating of the drill may result. If the drill is badly worn take a little of each side in turn until you make the final pass on each edge. The feed must not be further adjusted when making the final pass over the second edge. Should you be re-establishing a cutting edge on a broken drill then reshape the end by hand before using the jig.

FOUR FACET

I suspect the term "Four Facet" when applied to drills will be new to some readers, it is though, as the term implies, a drill sharpened with four faces rather than the normal two. This should not be confused with the drills available commercially which are known as having a "Split Point Geometry" even though there are similarities both in terms of shape and advantages, more about these later. It is an alternative method of sharpening drills in which each cutting lip has two flat surfaces, being primary and secondary clearance angles, similar to the cutting edges of an end mill.

9 Parts to assist in accurately rotating the drill by 180° for sharpening the second edge.

You may be tempted to say "so what" as the end away from the cutting edge is only clearance anyway. There is though a surprising effect of this method of sharpening and that is, the chisel edge is replaced by a point, see **SK7**. Advantages of a drill sharpened in this way is that the pressure required when drilling is reduced and with care will start without the need for center punching the hole position. On the downside the drills can be drawn into the material being drilled. This is especially so with materials that tend to draw the drill into it, some grades of brass typically.

While relatively easy to visualize, in practice it is more difficult to create and attempting this free hand is certainly a non starter as accuracy is more critical than with the conventional drill form. Sharpening drills to this form is

10 The parts in photograph 9 in use on the sharpening jig.

best done on a full function Tool and Cutter Grinder such as the Quorn, (Photo 4 Chapter 1) However, jigs have been developed which enable them to be sharpened using the simpler Worden grinder (Photo 6 Chapter 1) or similar.

The method most often put forward for sharpening drills in this way is to create the point using four flats. Having ground the first secondary angle it is then essential that the drill be rotated 180° and the second face ground at exactly the same depth. The primary angle is then ground in the same way, and again, both sides must be ground equally.

There is more to it than that, as not only must the two faces be ground at the same level this must also be chosen so that the four facets meet centrally at a point. It is therefore essential that both sides are ground equally but also that the amount removed produces the required point. This necessitates a little being removed from each side in turn until the required point is achieved. The process will therefore need some precise positioning to achieve the desired result.

The angles for the two facets for each edge should be around 10 degrees for the primary clearance and 25 degrees for the secondary, though like most things in metal cutting activities these values are not critical. I would though suggest that the secondary angle should be no less that 25 degrees, values between 25 degrees and 30 degrees being more appropriate. The other factor is how the secondary facet is positioned in relation to the primary. This should be done so that primary facet is a constant width from the center of the drill to the edge rather than triangular. For this to be achieved the drill is not rotated, to produce the second clearance, only the angle to the

wheel being increased. An accessory for carrying out this method of drill sharpening is detailed in Chapter 12 that also gives more technical data regarding this method of drill sharpening.

SPLIT POINT GEOMETRY

This is a form of drill that is now commercially quite common and has similarities with the four facet form, having both primary and secondary clearances. However, there are differences, one being that the primary facet has a triangular rather than a rectangular form. This can be seen by comparing **SK8** with **SK7**. Another difference is the secondary clearance has a much steeper angle of around 40°. It is also much more difficult to produce the secondary clearance.

In the case of the four facet method the drill can be just wiped across the flat face of a grinding wheel. This is not so in the case of a split point drill, as the secondary clearance must go only as far as the chisel edge so as to create a cutting edge on this as **SK8** attempts to illustrate.

The corner of the grinding wheel must therefore be used to produce this and it should be obvious that very accurate positioning is necessary. Also, the wheel must be dressed to have a sharp corner making it necessary to use a fine grit wheel especially if attempted to sharpen smaller drills.

The primary clearance can be produced using a conventional drill grinder but set to give a smaller chisel angle than normal of around 110 degrees. There is still yet another factor that must be observed when producing the secondary clearance. It can be seen from **SK8** that the primary facet has a triangular form.

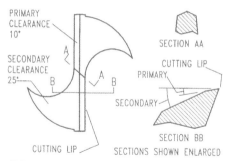

SK7. Four facet drill format.

THE PRIMARY CLEARANCE IS GROUND GENERALLY AS FOR A STANDARD DRILL FORM BUT WITH A GREATER EXTENSION FROM THE SHARPENING JIG SO AS TO PRODUCE A CHISEL ANGLE OF 110° PRIOR TO CREATING THE THIRD AND FOURTH FACETS

SK8. Split point drill form.

However, the angle of this cannot be chosen at random as it must rotate the chisel round to the standard angle of about 130 degrees, and yet there is more. The two secondary faces must not pass one another else you will end up with a forked point, it is advisable to avoid this by leaving just a small portion of the original chisel untouched, say about 0.1mm to 0.2mm wide.

The result of all these requirements is that sharpening this form of drill is far from straightforward and the four facet method that will cut almost as well will be the easier option. It is my understanding that the drill flute arrangement is identical to the standard drill. Therefore, if you come across any of these drills you can when blunt eventually sharpen them in the conventional form should you not want to attempt the split point geometry. **Photo 11** shows split point drills in close up.

POINT THINNING

Point thinning, seen illustrated in **SK9**, is useful on larger drills as it reduces the pressure required making it less of a strain on lightweight drilling machines. It can also be of help with drilling difficult materials, even when using smaller drills. You will need a wheel

with a very thin edge to do this even with drills of say 12mm (approx. ½") diameter, how practical it is to do this at smaller diameters will depend on the equipment available for carrying out the thinning. Thinning should be carried out equally on both flutes and central to the chisel, reducing the chisel to about 60 to 70% of its normal length.

For strength, the core thickness of a drill increases toward the drill shank, because of this a much shortened drill, maybe having been broken, may also require to have its point thinned.

DRILLING BRASS

Having said that four facet drills will tend to draw themselves into some grades of brass, the effect is not totally eliminated by the use of drills sharpened in the standard manner. To overcome the problem fully it is practice to remove the helix at the cutting edge by grinding a small flat as shown in **SK10**.

OTHER MATERIALS

While other forms of drills are supplied, typically slow spiral, and will work marginally better than the standard for some materials, the difference is small and the standard drills

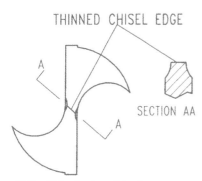

11 Split point drills

SK9. Chisel edge thinning.

will suffice for the type of work likely in the home workshop.

One area where there just may be an advantage in diverting from the standard is if you have a reoccurring task for drilling thin materials where the drill can start to break through before the hole has reached size on the front. Sharpening the drill with a flatter point will help to avoid this situation. The

modified drill will though have the problem of a curved cutting edge as mentioned. However, the curved edge can be removed while still maintaining the helix angle using a wheel with a narrow edge, see Chapter 1 Photo 9. It will though, not be a task to be carried out free hand.

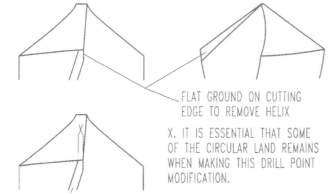

FLAT GROUND ON CUTTING EDGE TO REMOVE HELIX

X. IT IS ESSENTIAL THAT SOME OF THE CIRCULAR LAND REMAINS WHEN MAKING THIS DRILL POINT MODIFICATION.

SK10. Drill modification for drilling difficult materials.

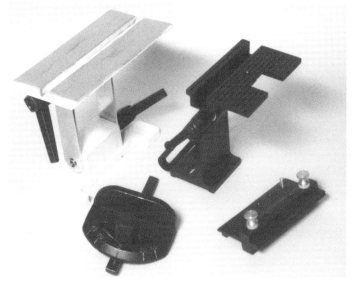

CHAPTER 3
GRINDING RESTS

In the last chapter it was described how twist drills could be sharpened using a standard bench grinder, assisted by a simple commercially available drill sharpening jig, also benched mounted. Unfortunately, especially if you are not into making workshop equipment, there are no comparable items for sharpening other metal working cutters, though a few do exist for woodworking tools. On the other hand, only simple shop made accessories are necessary for the majority of sharpening tasks required in the home workshop.

While having said that only simple accessories are necessary, this assumes that the bench grinder is further equipped with an improved grinding rest. **Photo 1** shows two commercially available rests that are a marked

1 Two commercially available rests.

2 A simple shop made rest. (Detailed in Chapter 9)

improvement over the rest supplied with a bench grinder. However, better rests can easily be shop made and are essential for the more complex sharpening requirements in the metalworking workshop, end mills typically.

The ability to control depth of cut is lacking in the commercial rests and the ability to set an angle to the side of the wheel. When sharpening the end teeth of an end mill, removing only sufficient to re-establish a sharp edge, and with all edges at the same level, will be the requirement. Depth of cut will

therefore need to be accurately controlled. Also, positioning the cutter relative to the grinding wheel will be critical to prevent the wheel touching the teeth that are not being ground at each stage. The rests in the photograph are therefore only suitable for woodworking tools.

Photo 2 shows a simple shop made grinding rest that meets the requirements as the following briefly explains. The table can be traversed towards and away (infeed) from the face of the wheel using the knob on the left. The total movement of the accessory being

3 An advanced grinding rest.

used is limited by the stop screw on the end of the fence, moving the table forward will therefore provide a greater depth of cut. The central knob is used to lock the table while grinding is taking place.

The knob on the right feeds the fence left and right (cross feed) and can control the amount being ground away if the tool being sharpened is passing down the side of the wheel. It can also precisely set the position of an end mill being sharpened on the face of the wheel so that the other cutting edges do not come into contact with it. These comments

should become much clearer when actual operations are explained later in the book. Details for making this rest are published in Chapter 9 together with the essential accessories in Chapters 10, 11 and 12. Most of the examples of tool sharpening in the book are illustrated using this rest.

An alternative to this is the rest seen in **Photo 3**, details of which are included in the book "Milling for Home Machinists." This rest has better facilities for positioning the item being sharpened and is in that respect an improvement over that in **Photo 2**. With this in mind it should be evident from the photograph that the crossfeed moves the table rather than just the fence as is the case with the simpler rest. However, in the case of the simper rest, coarse adjustment for moving the rest to and from the grinding wheel is linear, rather than on pivoted arms, and this makes it easier to set, as moving the rest does not affect its angle. An enterprising reader may like to marry the table of the rest in **Photo 3** with base of that in **Photo 2**.

The methods for using these two rests have some similarities with the methods for using the Worden (Photo 6) and the Kennet (Photo 7) both in Chapter 1. For example, having a table for support and the need for accessories to hold the cutter. The Worden and Kennet, being self-contained and having larger tables, will no doubt be a little easier to set up and use.

Before illustrating actual operations, some aspects of grinding must be understood. Two methods of applying the cutter to the wheel are possible.

1. To plunge the cutter onto the wheel's surface and remove.

2. To apply the cutter to the wheel moving it with a wiping action, either across the face or down the side of the wheel.

Method 1 has limited uses as it has the disadvantage that it will transfer irregularities on the wheel to the cutting edge being sharpened while method 2 will smooth them out. This though is an oversimplification, method 2 will only create a flat surface if the wiping action is done in a straight line, totally free hand grinding, even with a wiping action, cannot be guaranteed to produce a straight edge. Because of this, feed must be controlled, and in the case of the grinding

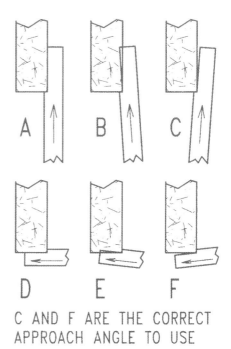

C AND F ARE THE CORRECT APPROACH ANGLE TO USE

SK1. Workpiece approach angle.

rests illustrated, a fence is used to guide the tool in a straight line.

Another aspect of this form of grinding is that grinding only takes place on the corner of the wheel. This is best understood by reference to **SK1**. The reader may be of the opinion that grinding will take place as illustrated by A and D, for this to work satisfactorily the approach angle would have to be set precisely parallel to the side or face of the wheel. As this level of precision cannot be guaranteed, an error may result in the condition illustrated in B and E with more being ground away than is required. For that

4 A Chisel being sharpened.

reason, the approach angle is deliberately set at an angle as is shown by C and F to avoid over grinding.

The angle should be as small as is practical while still ensuring that conditions A, B, D or E do not occur, one degree should be sufficient. This is not just a requirement in the home workshop due to the inability to work more accurately; it is also standard practice in industry for the same reasons.

However, with some wheel shapes when fitted to a tool and cutter grinder the angle can be created on the wheel by dressing it accordingly. Of course, the item may pass down the left side of the wheel or be fed left to right on the face of the wheel where this is beneficial.

It may be considered that the fence on the rest's table would be used to establish the angle required on the sharpened tool,

5 Cardboard gauges for setting grinding rest.

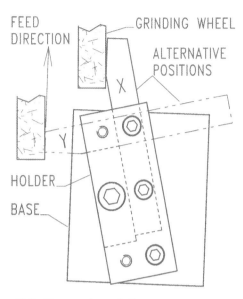

FEED DIRECTION

GRINDING WHEEL

ALTERNATIVE POSITIONS

X

Y

HOLDER

BASE

SK2. Sharpening a lathe roughing tool.

that is not so, its purpose is purely to set the approach angle. The tool must be set at an angle on the accessory's swivel base to achieve the tool's required angle, **Photo 4** shows how both angles are achieved. I have chosen to publish a photograph of a chisel being sharpened as the large angle required illustrates the situation more clearly. It can be seen from this that the fence sets the angle at which the face being sharpened passes the side of the wheel, while the angle that the chisel is set on the base controls the angle ground. See also **SK2** that shows two faces of a lathe roughing tool being ground.

The two rests (**Photo's 2 and 3**) incorporate fine feed adjustments both to and from the face of the wheel (infeed) and also the side of the wheel (crossfeed). In the case of the set up for sharpening the chisel, the crossfeed adjustment will initially be set to ensure that only a very small amount is ground away. If after a few passes the chisel is inspected and found in need of more being removed the fence can be moved over, say 0.001", and additional passes made. This will be repeated until the required face results.

SETTING THE ANGLE

As has already been said, a sharp cutter with an imperfect angle will be far better than a blunt cutter with a better angle. Only one thing is absolutely essential and that is that there should be an angle to provided clearance in front of the cutting edge, if this is not provided a cutter cannot cut, see **SK3**.

However, even though there is some tolerance as to the angles ground it will be good practice to make the settings to known values, rather than casually to an angle that looks about right. You will then have

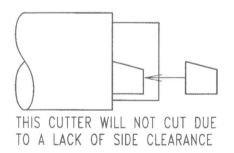

THIS CUTTER WILL NOT CUT DUE TO A LACK OF SIDE CLEARANCE

SK3. Zero clearance.

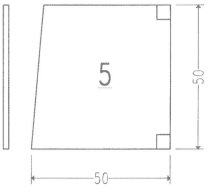

MAKE GAUGES FOR TYPICALLY 1,
2, 3, 4, 5, 6, 8, 10, 12, 15,
20 AND 25 DEGREES

MATERIAL
GOOD QUALITY CARD
OR ALUMINIUM 1 – 2mm THICK

QUANTITY
1 OFF EACH ANGLE REQUIRED

SK4. Angle gauges.

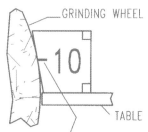

MARK GAUGE AT HEIGHT AT
WHICH GRINDING IS TO TAKE
PLACE

SK6. Angle to face of wheel.

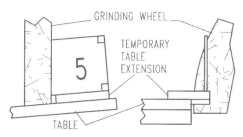

SK5. Angle to side of wheel.

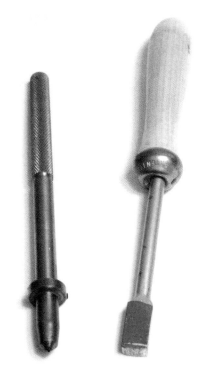

6 Wheel dressers, left single diamond, right multi diamond.

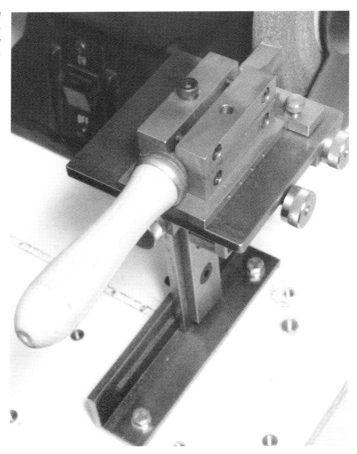

7 Multi diamond dresser in use being held in a holder and guided by the rest mounted fence.

knowledge of actual angles ground on which you can base other tasks in the future. As an aid to setting the angles, gauges should be made as those shown in **Photo 5** and **SK4**.

Using these to set the angle to the side of the wheel is straightforward but as the rest does not pass down the side of the wheel a small temporary table extension will be required as illustrated by **SK5**.

Working on the face of the wheel will result in the ground surface being concave though in most cases this is of little consequence due to the narrowness of the face produced. More important, the angle will depend on the height above the table and because of this it must be set at the height at which grinding is to take place, see **SK6**. This aspect of sharpening will become more apparent when actual applications are explained.

WHEEL DRESSING

Wheels are dressed for two reasons. On initial fitting, it is necessary to dress the wheel to ensure that it is running true, else off hand grinding will be difficult to control. Also, in addition to vibration of the workpiece, the grinder itself may also shake. Subsequently, after use, the wheel will require dressing to re-establish its cutting efficiency.

Photo 6 shows two items for dressing wheels, that on the left has a single large diamond brazed into its end. This is lightly passed over the wheel's surface to break away the worn abrasive particles and to reveal a fresh surface. That on the right of the photograph works in much the same way but has many smaller diamonds embedded in a soft metal head, as diamonds break away fresh diamonds become available.

These dressers can be used free hand and will give reasonable results if used in this way. It is though preferable to use them guided to ensure a flat surface results. The photograph shows that the single diamond has a collar on its stem that can be guided by the fence on the rest's table. The collar is movable to cope with variations in the distance between fence and wheel. An alternative, and better approach, is to mount either form of dresser in a holder and use this as illustrated in **Photo 7**, note the fence on the table that is being used to guide the holder is set left to right. The table infeed controls how much is removed. The holder in **Photo 7** is detailed in Chapter 11.

Another form of wheel dresser has a number of star shaped wheels that rotate as they are applied to the wheel. This has the effect of breaking away blunt particles to reveal a new surface. However, while these have the advantage of being cheaper it will be difficult to ensure that a flat surface is being produced, they are also mainly intended for larger wheels.

IMPORTANT SAFETY REQUIREMENTS

As with all workshop machinery, using grinding equipment requires that safety be given due consideration. While the following has been written with the two featured rests in mind it will generally apply to all forms of cutter grinding equipment.

- Do wear safety glasses or a facemask.
- Due to the item being ground often being unsupported close to the wheel when using the accessories, take only very light cuts. The depth of cut must be controlled by the fine feeds and the fence rather than manually.
- Make multiple passes where more than can be taken safely at a single pass has to be removed.
- Keep the overhang of the tool from the accessory holding it to a minimum.
- In view of the overhang, do ensure the accessory is held firmly down on the rest's table.
- The rest can be used as a conventional off hand grinding rest, in which case ensure that the front edge of the table is no more than 1mm from the grinding wheel and the item being ground supported by the rest's table.

- When the grinder is running, DO NOT make adjustments to the rest, other than using the fine feeds.
- Other than the fine feeds, make sure that all other adjustments are firmly locked before starting the grinder.
- As the grinding rest is not directly mounted off the grinder itself, it is essential that both be mounted on a very robust base. If this is not done the rest will be able to flex on its mounting relative to the off hand grinder when in use. At best, this may result in inaccurate results, but much worse, be the cause of a serious accident.

SOME TIPS FOR USING THE RESTS

Keep the table and the sliding surfaces of the accessory as free of grinding dust as possible resulting in easier hand feeding and making for safer working.

Remember the accessory will pick up particles from the workbench.

Use a small soft brush, typically a 1" paintbrush, to remove grinding dust from the table and accessory's base. This will make a very noticeable improvement to the ease of feeding the accessory.

In the same way as your cutting tools will need sharpening, so will your grinding wheel, dressing this frequently will make a very noticeable improvement.

Dust from the dressing operation will be more destructive than that produced during normal use. Therefore, if the grinder is on a separate base rather than bench mounted, move the grinder outside the workshop for the dressing operation. If not possible, a vacuum cleaner should be set running with its hose suitably positioned adjacent to the grinder. The hose should ideally be a large diameter one and must be firmly anchored or held by an assistant. If the approach angle is correct, sparks will only be seen coming from the corner of the wheel. Checking that this is the case will prove that the angle has been set correctly. Good lighting for carrying out sharpening operations is essential.

HAVE PATIENCE; setting up is time consuming as there are many adjustments to be set before sharpening can take place. This will still be the case even if using a dedicated tool and cutter grinder, such as the Quorn, maybe even more so due to their complexity.

Because of the above, obtain more than one of the most used end mills, blunt end mills can then be kept and sharpened as a batch.

When creating your own special set ups, that is other than those illustrated in the book, endeavour to ensure that the fence is between the wheel and the accessory. With this situation, if the accessory moves from the fence the cutter will move from the wheel and have less ground from it than is required. It can then be returned and reground. If the accessory is between the fence and the wheel it will be easy for too much to be ground away.

CHAPTER 4
SHARPENING LATHE TOOLS

Lathe tools without doubt provide the most diverse range of sharpening requirements in the home workshop; fortunately, it's mostly straightforward and quite tolerant of deviations from the ideal. It is also in many cases relatively easy to produce a working tool using free hand methods. That having been said, using only very simple accessories will improve the end result appreciably. Typically, the assembly illustrated in **SK1** is all that is necessary for sharpening the vast majority of lathe tools when used with a suitable grinding rest. Free hand sharpening should be reserved for that very special tool that is difficult to produce by any other method available in the average home

1 A Radius tool is one tool that will have to be sharpened free hand. The round diamond file will help to finalize the shape.

workshop. The radius forming tool seen in **Photo 1** is a typical example.

Even with the increased use of replaceable tip tooling there are still requirements that cannot be met by using this type of cutter. Typically, it is very difficult to make and fit very small tips, say for a very small boring tool. Special form tooling, such as required for cutting an acme thread or a worm gear are other instances of the need to use traditional HSS tooling. In some cases, tipped tools may be available for the task in hand but if having limited use, then the expense of purchasing a holder and tip may not be justifiable.

Another factor is that the material used cannot be honed to a very fine edge that is necessary to enable very shallow cuts to be taken when attempting to work to extremely close tolerances. **Photo 2** shows (well it is under there somewhere) a round nose tool being use to size a number of hole gauges where the swarf produced is more like grinding particles, this would not be possible with a standard tipped tool. Incidentally, the tool had become magnetized hence the build up of swarf. Working with magnetized tools is not to be recommended but it illustrates nicely what can be achieved with a finely honed lathe tool.

Because of these and other factors, sharpening lathe tools will be a requirement in the home workshop for many years to come.

As already said, lathe tooling is one area where free hand sharpening can often produce a working tool. While this is so, the accessories required are so simple and the end result so much improved that there really is no justification for attempting it. Also, using some simple accessory to hold and guide the tool is far safer than the totally free hand method.

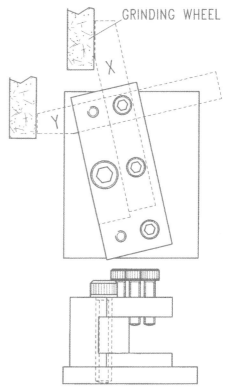

GRINDING WHEEL

X. POSITION FOR SHARPENING SIDE AND TOP CLEARANCES AND RELIEF.
Y. POSITION FOR SHARPENING FRONT CLEARANCE AND RELIEF.

ASSEMBLY COMPRISES SQUARE WORKPIECE HOLDER AND SWIVEL BASE

SK1. Square workpiece holder assembly.

2 A finely honed HSS tool is capable of taking very shallow cuts producing swarf like grinding dust.

KNIFE TOOL

Photo 3 shows a knife tool being sharpened using a simple rest and an accessory for holding the tool. Three angles have to be set up to before starting to sharpen this tool.

1. The table is tilted, left to right, to establish the side clearance (3) (see SK3 also SK2 for definitions), setting the angle as shown in SK5 Chapter 3.

2. The fence is set so that the tool passes the side of the wheel, grinding only on the corner of the wheel. Again refer to Chapter 3 SK1c.

3. The angle of the side relief (6) is set by the position of the tool holder on the swivel base. The fence angle has been deliberately increased in the photograph, from the 1 to 2 degrees required, to make it apparent. **SK3** also shows a knife tool but this one without side relief (6).

The cap head screw, far right of the fence, acts as a stop for the base ensuring that grinding ceases at the same position at each pass. However, adjusting the infeed that moves the table towards and away from the wheel face sets the actual position that the base stops relative to the wheel. The crossfeed movement of the fence sets the amount ground from the tool itself. To limit the heat generated the amount ground at each stage should be kept low; say 0.001". Traverse the tool back and forth a few times until the amount of sparks produced diminishes appreciably. Inspect the result and repeat as necessary with further cuts of 0.001".

Using the design of rest seen in the photograph it is inevitable that there will be some play at the end of the fence due to clearance in its slide, but with care in manufacture this should not create a problem. It is though, good practice to ease

SK2. Cutter angles.

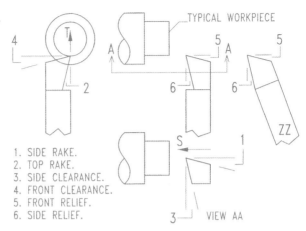

1. SIDE RAKE.
2. TOP RAKE.
3. SIDE CLEARANCE.
4. FRONT CLEARANCE.
5. FRONT RELIEF.
6. SIDE RELIEF.

VIEW AA

NOTES
A. FOR CLARITY OF DRAWING, ANGLES ARE SHOWN GREATER THAN IS NORMALLY REQUIRED.
B. THE ANGLES SHOWN ARE RELATIVE TO THE WORKPIECE AND EACH OTHER AND NOT TO THE SHANK. IF THE TOOL IS TO BE SET ROUND, AS FOR THE AMERICAN TOOL POST, THE TOOL WILL APPEAR WITH SHANK AS AT ZZ.
C. TOP RAKE(2) IS MOSTLY USED FOR TOOLS WHICH FEED IN THE DIRECTION OF ARROW T AND SIDE RAKE(1) FOR TOOLS WHICH FEED IN THE DIRECTION OF ARROW S.

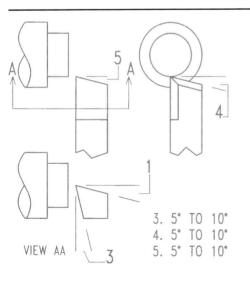

VIEW AA

SK3. Knife tool

3. 5° TO 10°
4. 5° TO 10°
5. 5° TO 10°

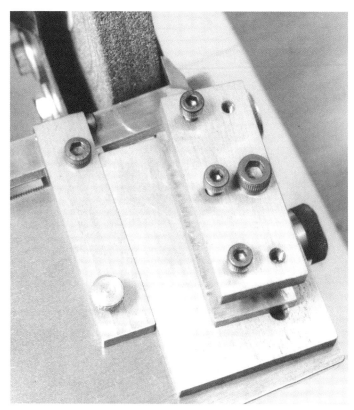

the end of the fence consistently in the same direction while making each adjustment and prior to locking it with the locking screw, seen bottom left of the fence. The design for this rest is given in Chapter 9.

The above procedure will in general apply to virtually all lathe tools with only minor variations to the process, further detailed descriptions are therefore unnecessary, a few additional photographs will though help to emphasize the method of working.

Photo 4 shows a roughing tool being ground, this time using the more complex rest. This clearly shows that the table is tilted to provide the side relief and that the holder

is at an angle on the base to set the roughing tool side relief (negative in this case), see **SK4**. The photograph also shows that there is no stop screw at the end of the fence, with the roughing tool shape this is not necessary. However, it clearly shows how this table can be moved left/right by the addition of the dovetail slide in that direction. Therefore, the table, with the fence, move together for setting depth of cut on the side of the wheel, rather than just the fence as is the case with the simpler rest detailed extensively in this book. Details of the advanced rest are given in the Workshop Practice series, Ref. 1.

4 Sharpening a roughing tool on the more complex rest.

Roughing tools have a generous radius between the side relief (6) and the front relief (5). This is best produced freehand as described later for a round nose tool.

ACME AND WORM WHEEL CUTTER

Other cutters that will use essentially the same processes are those required for cutting an acme thread or a worm wheel. These are best ground using a round tool bit enabling them to be rotated to suit the helix angle of the worm or thread being cut. When in use these tools are held in a holder specifically for the tool as seen in **Photo 5**.

This is also ideal for holding the tool while being ground as can be seen in **Photo 6**.

An essential feature of these tools, **SK5**, is the setting face ground on the side. This makes it possible to check that the tool when being used has been rotated in its holder to suit the helix angle of the workpiece being made. The angle, being dependent on both diameter and pitch, is as a result a variable.

Having first ground the flat, grinding the left side will replicate the process above for the roughing tool (**Photo 4**) while for the right side the table will be tilted the other way, the holder repositioned on the base, and the tool passed down the left side of the wheel. The

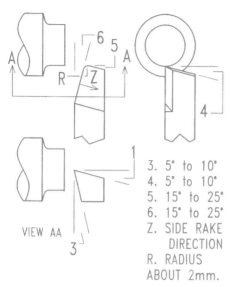

3. 5° to 10°
4. 5° to 10°
5. 15° to 25°
6. 15° to 25°
Z. SIDE RAKE
   DIRECTION
R. RADIUS
   ABOUT 2mm.

VIEW AA

SK4. Roughing tool.

angle of the tool on the base will of course be quite critical for tools of this type, though with a suitable protractor, it's not that difficult to set sufficiently accurate. Do remember that the angle of the fence has no bearing on the angle ground.

Photo 7, shows the front clearance (4) being ground by plunging it onto the side of the wheel. The stop at the end of the fence, together with the rest's infeed, is used to establish the width of the tip. As the width is important the infeed is advanced a little at a time until the required width results.

The photograph shows that the rest has been repositioned at the side of the wheel and while this position has limited use provisions for mounting the rest in this way should be made for the occasional use.

It should be obvious that the helix setting flat, the two sides and the end, must all be made without moving the cutter in its holder, only the table angles being changed. At this stage I should add that it will be necessary to refer to data published elsewhere (Typically Ref. 2) for details of cutter angles, tip widths, etc. and essential information regarding how these thread forms are machined.

It still remains to create the top rake (2). Having accurately ground the two side faces to the internal angle required it should be understood that including a top rake will

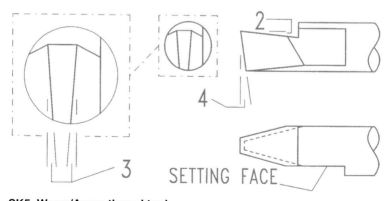

SETTING FACE

SK5. Worm/Acme thread tool.

have the effect of altering the angle, actually making the internal angle smaller. Working with a zero degree top rake would avoid the error but this would reduce its cutting efficiently.

Fortunately, only a few degrees rake will significantly increase cutting efficiency while having only limited effect on the resultant angle. I would therefore suggest a compromise angle of five degrees for the top rake irrespective of the material being machined.

Theoretically, it would be possible to calculate the change in angle due to adding top rake but the change would be so small as to be impossible to work to with equipment available in the home workshop. My only suggestion is that you should ensure that the angles set for the sides of the tool do not start on the low side.

While not shown on **SK5** a few degrees side rake could also be incorporated. In this case the tool would be fed in at an angle so

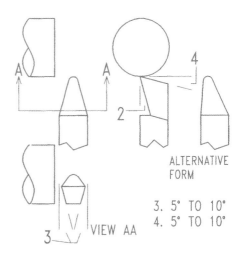

ALTERNATIVE FORM

3. 5° TO 10°
4. 5° TO 10°

SK6. Round nose tool.

that it cuts only on the end and the one side. Again, refer to Ref. 2. Actually, the process of grinding the top rake and side rake (if any) would closely follow that for the knife tool, **Photo 3**.

5 Tool for cutting an Acme thread.

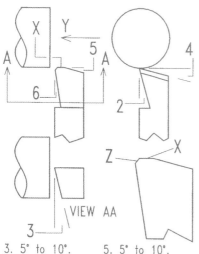

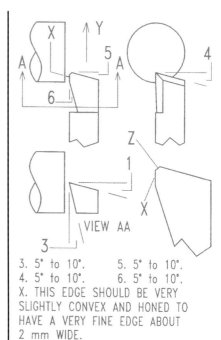

3. 5° to 10°.   5. 5° to 10°.
4. 5° to 10°.   6. 5° to 10°.
X. THIS EDGE SHOULD BE VERY
SLIGHTLY CONVEX AND HONED TO
HAVE A VERY FINE EDGE ABOUT
2 mm WIDE.
Z. CHAMFER ABOUT 1 mm
Y. DIRECTION OF FEED.

SK7. Outside diameter finishing tool.

3. 5° to 10°.   5. 5° to 10°.
4. 5° to 10°.   6. 5° to 10°.
X. THIS EDGE SHOULD BE VERY
SLIGHTLY CONVEX AND HONED TO
HAVE A VERY FINE EDGE ABOUT
2 mm WIDE.
Z. CHAMFER ABOUT 1 mm
Y. DIRECTION OF FEED.

SK8. Face finishing tool.

ROUND NOSE TOOLS (SK6)

Rather like the form tool in Photo 1, the external radius of the round nose tool is a shape that has to be largely achieved free hand. However, an extension table to the side of the wheel, set to the appropriate angle, enables the side clearance (3) and the front clearance (4) to be accurately maintained as the tool is rotated to produce the round end, **Photo 8**.

THE SKETCHES

Some explanation is necessary regarding the sketches, 1 to 6 already having been briefly mentioned but with sketches 7 to 10 showing additional types of tools. **SK2**

is a hypothetical tool that illustrates the six angles and their names, some of which that will occur on each form of lathe tool. The numbers, 1 Side rake, 2 Top rake, etc. are used consistently on all the other sketches and throughout this chapter. It will be found that when studying them that values are only quoted for angles 3, 4, 5 and 6. This is because angles 1 and 2 depend on the material being machined. That having been said, for low volume production, where machining rates and tool life are less important, the angles are far from critical.

Most of the sketches quote angles of 5 to 10 degrees for the clearance and relief angles, and in the home workshop, working towards the lower value would be a good course of action, as this will give a more robust cutting edge.

As the swarf being produced has to slide over the side and top rakes, it should be obvious that the steeper the angle the easier will the material be cut. However, this is an oversimplification. A steeper angle will obviously result in a finer, but weaker, edge, and a compromise is therefore necessary between ease of cut and staying power of the tool's edge.

The following gives an indication of suitable rake angles though there are many grades for a given metal that will theoretically have some bearing on the angle chosen. As I have already said though, quite wide variations in angle will still give a tool that is adequate for the home workshop. A SHARP EDGE IS FAR MORE IMPORTANT THAN THE PRECISE ANGLE CHOSEN.

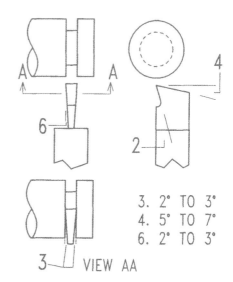

3. 2° TO 3°
4. 5° TO 7°
6. 2° TO 3°

VIEW AA

SK9. Parting off tool.

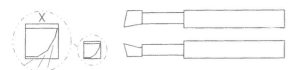

X. SHOWS HOW FRONT CLEARANCE IS GRADUALLY INCREASED TO ENABLE THE TOOL TO BE USED AT THE SMALLEST POSSIBLE DIAMETER. OTHER ANGLES CONFORM GENERALLY TO THOSE FOR OUTSIDE DIAMETER TURNING.

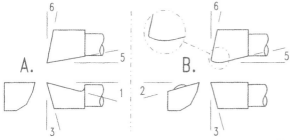

SK10. Boring tools.

A. GENERAL PURPOSE BORING TOOL, ALSO FACES THE BOTTOM OF BLIND, OR SEMI BLIND HOLES.
B. INSIDE DIAMETER FINISHING TOOL, CONFORMS CLOSELY TO REQUIREMENTS FOR THE OUTSIDE DIAMETER FINISHING TOOL.

6 Sharpening an Acme tool in the same holder as would be used to hold the tool on the lathes top slide.

Free cutting mild steel	20 - 25
Aluminum	20 - 25
Copper	20 - 25
Mild steel	10 - 15
Cast iron	5 - 10
Drill rod and similar	5 - 10
Stainless	5 - 10
Brass, gun metal, etc.	0 - 2
Plastics	0 - (-10)

Just in case you think that it may be a printing error, the minus 10 degrees quoted for plastic is correct, a negative side/top rake (1/2) is often found advantageous with some plastic materials.

The shapes shown in the sketches are typical and there is much room for variation, the knife tool being sharpened in **Photo 3** compared to knife tool in **SK3** being a typical example.

7 Sharpening the end of an Acme tool on the side of a wheel. This is one case where mounting the rest on the side of a wheel is beneficial.

8 Free hand sharpening of the end radius of a round nose tool using a side table extension.

SHARPENING VERSUS SHAPING

The explanations given so far are really intended for tools just having the cutting edges sharpened and in which case only a very small amount will require removing. In this case overheating of the tool bit should not be a problem.

However, frequently the tool will initially have to be shaped from a blank and in this case overheating is a distinct possibility. In the commercial set up, grinding will be done under a generous flow of coolant to avoid this. As this will be impracticable, grinding needs to be done a little at a time and allowed to cool between stages.

Under no circumstances should the tool, be it a lathe tool, drill, or an end mill be plunged into a coolant, as this may cause the cutting edge to crack. The most that can be done is to place the tool on a block of steel to act as a heat sink to speed up cooling.

Even if done free hand it will be an advantage in most cases to hold the tool blank in the accessory used for sharpening, as this will give a larger item to hold and as a result be a safer operation.

BORING TOOLS

When dealing with outside diameter turning a very small number of tools will satisfy almost all OD turning requirements. In fact, a basic knife tool will work with any diameter and

length while also being able to machine end faces. This single tool could as a result satisfy the needs of say 99% of outside diameter work, albeit not ideally. This is far from the case in boring tools that must be available in various sizes to cope with differing diameters and depth, possibly with additional forms for through and blind holes. **Photo 9** shows some typical examples.

The subject of this book, being the sharpening of workshop tooling, it is not appropriate to go into great depth regarding the wide variety of boring tools used, if you need further details then a book relating to the use of the lathe would be a good starting point. However, despite the wide range of sizes required, the actual cutting edges conform very closely to those in **SK2** but with one exception. With a tool intended for outside diameter turning the curvature of the part being turned further increase the clearance provided by the front clearance (5). This is not the case with a boring tool where the curvature of the hole reduces the relief, see **SK10**.

Despite the more complex shape of the main portion of a boring tool, the sharpening operations can still easily be accomplished using the techniques described above, as illustrated in **Photo 10**. This shows the side clearance (3) being sharpened on the face of the wheel. The result will be a concave face

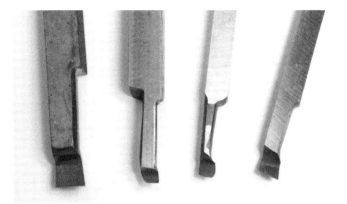

9 Typical boring tools for use on the lathe.

SECTIONS

1. SHAPE SIDE OF SHANK
2. SHAPE BELOW SHANK
3. RADIUS SHANK

4. MAKE FRONT END CLEARANCE

5. MAKE TOP RAKE

6. MAKE SECONDARY FRONT CLEARANCE

7. MAKE FRONT CLEARANCE

THE DIAGRAMS ARE DIAGRAMATIC ONLY, CORNERS WILL NOT BE SHARP AS SHOWN.

THE SUGGESTED METHOD IS FOR GUIDANCE ONLY THERE IS MUCH FREEDOM TO VARY METHOD AND SHAPE TO SUIT.

SK11. Shaping boring tools.

but at this diameter of wheel the effect is minimal. From the photograph it can be seen that the fence is set left to right and the tool is ground with a wiping action, as it is traversed along the fence. The amount ground away is controlled by the infeed.

Initial shaping of a boring tool from a high speed steel blank is a time consuming exercise and must be done with care, **SK11** shows a typical sequence. Again, this is best done with the tool blank held in the holder. If you have hardening and tempering equipment and experience you may like to shape a tool from drill rod while still soft rather than a HSS blank. However, the lasting power of the eventual edge will not be that of a HSS cutter that will last a lifetime if used and sharpened with care.

MILLING CUTTERS

While the above has emphasized lathe tooling, some tools for use on the milling machine, fly cutters, tools for boring heads, etc. will use similar sharpening techniques. These though invariably have round shanks and for these to be held the round workpiece holder, SK1 Chapter 7, should be used.

10 Sharpening a boring tool using a square tool holder, a left to right mounted fence and the simple rest.

Photo 11 shows this on its swivel base, being used while sharpening a boring tool for use on a milling machine. Details for making the round workpiece holder are given in Chapter 11.

REFERENCES

1. "Milling for Home Machinists."

2. "Screw Cutting in the Lathe." Workshop Practice Series, Number 3.

3. "Gears and Gear Cutting." Workshop Practice Series, Number 17.

11 Sharpening a boring head boring tool using the round workpiece holder.

CHAPTER 5

SHARPENING END MILLS

Considering the large amount of use an end mill gets in the modern home workshop it is probably the most neglected of all the common cutting tools used. This situation, without doubt, is due to the lack of equipment capable of carrying out the sharpening tasks required. However, while sharpening the side cutting edges requires quite precise equipment, the end teeth can be sharpened with only the minimum.

Sketch **SK1** shows that no matter how wide a step is being cut the end tooth only cuts on its tip and at a width less than the feed rate per tooth. Therefore, if the cutter is only being used for surfacing, **SK1.1**, sharpening just the end teeth will appreciably improve the cutter's performance. If a cutter is reserved purely for this operation then the small radius that will be develop between the end and side edges, on a blunt cutter, will be removed by sharpening just the end teeth.

Even if the cutter is to be used for cutting a step, **SK1.2** sharpening just the end teeth will improve the situation a little but there is no real alternative but to sharpen the side also.

Fortunately, in the case of milling cutters, in the home workshop there are only a small

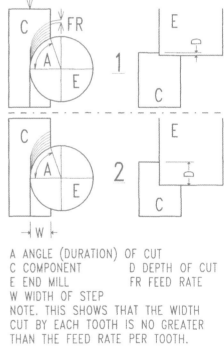

A ANGLE (DURATION) OF CUT
C COMPONENT   D DEPTH OF CUT
E END MILL   FR FEED RATE
W WIDTH OF STEP
NOTE. THIS SHOWS THAT THE WIDTH CUT BY EACH TOOTH IS NO GREATER THAN THE FEED RATE PER TOOTH.

SK1. End mill tooth load.

1 Sharpening the end teeth of an end mill using a simple square holder and plunging the cutter into the curved face of the grinding wheel.

number of shank diameters, 6, 8, 10, 12 and 16 millimeter for metric, and ¼", ⅜", ½" and ⅝" in the imperial sizes. Because of this the number of holders or collets to be made to enable the sharpening to take place is not that great.

THE END TEETH

By far the simplest method of sharpening the end teeth is to use a square holder, bored to be a close fit on the cutter's shank and fitted with a grub screw (setscrew), to hold the cutter in place, **SK2**. The square can then be used to index the cutter for sharpening the four edges in turn, as shown in **Photo 1**. In this situation, the fence is used to guide the holder while the cutter is plunged into the wheel's face, using the stop screw and infeed to control the amount ground away.

The four teeth are ground in turn and the cutter inspected, if the result needs more to be removed the infeed is adjusted a little, say 0.001", and the four edges ground again.

The left to right adjustment also needs setting so that the full width of the tooth is ground but ensuring that the wheel does not

BORE TO BE CENTRAL IN SQUARE AND A CLOSE FIT ON THE END MILL SHANK. FIT GRUB SCREW FOR HOLDING END MILL

SK2. End mill holder.

2 Grinding a cross on the end of an end mill to relieve the center once sharpening of the end teeth has resulted in the center impression being eliminated.

contact the others. Setting the angle of the fence should be done such that the resulting edges are concave, **SK3**. This is essential so that the cutter only contacts the workpiece at the outer end of the teeth. Setting the fence at about 1 to 2 degrees will suffice.

The angle at the point on the wheel's face at which sharpening is to take place should be set to 5 degrees, see Chapter 3, SK6. After repeated sharpening, the width of the primary clearance will become too great, say 0.08" or more, and the secondary clearance will require attention. Do this, using the same method but with the angle set to between 10 and 12 degrees, reducing the width of the primary clearance to about 0.04". This will give scope for further sharpening before the secondary clearance will again need grinding.

Eventually the center hole of the cutter will be ground away and some form of relieving its center will be required. Ideally a small grinding point in a high-speed grinder could be plunged in to re-establish the indent. However, the facility for carrying out this task is unlikely to be available in the majority of workshops and some other method will have to be found. An easy method is to set the cutter at 45 degrees in the holder and use this to create a cross using the corner of the wheel as shown in **Photos 2** and **3**. This method, though crude, is adequate as the cutter cuts only on the tips of the end teeth.

A tidier method would be to use a saucer wheel with its thin edge to create the cross; it would though be impractical to keep changing the wheels on the workshop's off hand grinder for these specialist tasks. However, in Chapter

13, a modification to a basic bench grinder is suggested so that this can be reserved for all cutter sharpening.

If you chose to make the accessory for sharpening the side teeth (Chapter 10) then this can also be used to hold the cutter while sharpening the end teeth, the process being essentially the same, but more details later in the chapter.

THE SIDE CUTTING EDGES

Sharpening the side cutting edges of an end mill is almost certainly the most demanding sharpening task likely to surface in the average home workshop, as complex, if not more, than sharpening reamers and taps. However, the need to sharpen end mills will be an absolute certainty while in the case of reamers and taps most workshops will get by without the need. It is therefore essential to provide a facility for carrying out this task, That is, unless you have your cutters sharpened professionally, or chose to get by with blunt cutters, eventually replacing them with new ones before their time.

If you equip yourself with a Quorn or a Stent it is likely that you will also make an accessory specifically to suit the particular machine, alternatively you may choose to purchase a commercially available accessory to use. Whatever approach you take there is likely to be very little difference with the basic design of the unit.

This book primarily attempts to carry out the required sharpening applications with the minimum of equipment but for this task there really is no alternative but to make available an accessory comparable to those used with the Quorn, Stent, or even a full function industrial tool and cutter grinder. Whether you make

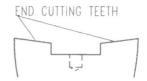

END CUTTING TEETH

END TEETH OF AN END MILL MUST BE CONCAVE. SKETCH SHOWS ONLY TWO TEETH. ANGLE SHOULD BE 1 TO 2° SHOWN EXAGERATED FOR CLARITY.

SK3. End mill end tooth form.

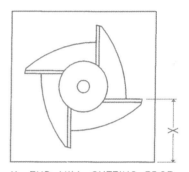

X. END MILL CUTTING EDGE PARALLEL WITH BASE POSITION FOR GRINDING

SK4. End teeth.

3 The result of the operation in Photo 2.

4 The end mill accessory, the most complex in this book, but essential for sharpening the side teeth of an end mill.

this, or purchase a commercial item, the task of sharpening the cutter will be the same.

Essentially, the process is to move the end mill along the grinding wheel at the same time rotating it so that the wheel remains in contact with the edge being sharpened. However, having now introduced this accessory, I will deal with using it first for the end teeth and then the side cutting edges. The explanations will largely be appropriate to other similar units also.

END TEETH

Fit the accessory, **Photo 4**, with the four tooth indexing collar, ensuring that there is no end float and adjust the bearings so that the spindle rotates freely but without shake.

Fit the end mill making sure that the end teeth cutting edges are horizontal and vertical, **SK4,** when the index collar is located against the index arm, and lock the spindle.

Set the end mill accessory on the swivel base to an angle of approximately 1 to 2

degrees to ensure that the end teeth when ground will be slightly concave, see earlier **SK3.** Fit the fence to the table, with the stop screw at the left hand end, and at an angle of 1 to 2 degrees relative to the face of the wheel to ensure grinding takes place on the wheel's right corner only. Set the table at approximately 90 degrees to the side of the wheel and about 5 degrees relative to its face, doing this at the point where grinding will take place. With the swivel base against the fence and the stop, and the end mill very close to the face of the wheel, adjust the cross traverse such that when grinding the wheel will not touch the adjacent end teeth. Err on the side of caution, fine adjustment is carried out once grinding takes place. At this stage the adjustments are made with the grinder at rest. Do not forget to make sure that all coarse adjustments are firmly locked and do a few dummy runs to get the feel of the operation before turning the grinder on.

5 Sharpening the end teeth with a wiping action rather than being plunged into the wheel as in Photo 1. The stop screw seen on the fence prevents the wheel from contacting the three edges not being ground.

With the grinder running and the swivel base held firmly against the fence and stop, very slowly advance the infeed until the first sparks appear. Move the end mill to the right and using the infeed place on a very small cut, about 0.001". Now slowly feed the end mill to the left until the stop is reached, **Photo 5**, ensuring that the swivel base is being held firmly against the fence and the tabletop during the operation. Remove the assembly from the table and check to see if the whole length of the end tooth has been ground and the adjacent end tooth not touched. Make adjustments to the cross traverse if necessary.

It is perhaps a point in the book where it is worth commenting on the major advantage of using a fence in the way that all the

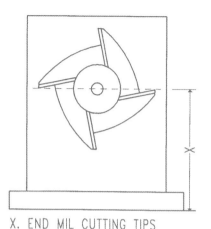

X. END MIL CUTTING TIPS
PARALLEL WITH BASE

SK5. Position for grinding outer edges.

operations in the book propose. I have emphasized the need to keep the swivel base firmly against the fence. However, if this is not done, too little, rather than too much, will be removed from the cutter being sharpened. It will then be possible to return and traverse the cutter across the wheel once more to achieve the desired result. If the accessory were between the fence and the wheel it would be possible to grind too much from the cutter being ground.

Having ground the first edge and without making further adjustments, rotate the end mill ensuring that it is locked at each position and grind the remaining three edges. Inspect the result and if necessary slightly advance the infeed and regrind all four teeth, repeat until a satisfactory result is achieved. Remember to make only very small adjustments between each grinding. Comments made earlier in the chapter regarding primary and secondary angles and widths still apply.

It would of course also be possible to use the accessory in the same way as the square

holders and just plunge the cutter into the face of the wheel. On the other hand, you may wonder why when using the square holder the cutter is not wiped across the wheel rather than plunging it. This is because, in my estimation, it would be difficult to reliably keep the narrow end of the holder in contact with the fence while carrying out the wiping action. With the wider swivel base this is not a problem.

CUTTING EDGES

Swing the index arm away from the index collar, which should also be loosened and moved towards the end of the spindle. Fix the collar at a position that will enable the spindle to move lengthwise by an amount approximately 0.2" greater than the length of the end mill's cutting edges. The spindle must slide through the bearings easily but without any shake. An essential requirement for this to be achieved is for the spindle to be thoroughly cleaned of all grinding dust. Do not be tempted to lubricate the assembly, as the oil will only retain any grinding dust that lands on the spindle.

Fit the tooth rest support to support the end mill at its outer end and adjust the height so that the opposing end teeth tips are horizontal, **SK5, Photo 6**. Note that this is subtly different to the setting for sharpening the end teeth, compare **SK4** with **SK5**. This set-up can be done with the accessory away from the grinding rest.

As grinding is taking place on the outer diameter the clearance needs to vary depending on the cutter's diameter, rather like a boring tool would for a small diameter hole. As a guide the angles should vary from 15 degrees at ¼" diameter to 5 degrees at ¾" diameter and above. The angles are not

Above: 6 Setting up the end mill accessory for sharpening the side teeth, see SK5. Right: 7. End mill accessory in use on the rest. Note the cutter is on the left of wheel with the fence on the right. This is opposite to the set up for most sharpening tasks.

crucial so interpolating for intermediate values will suffice and if in doubt err a degree or two on the high side.

While 5 degrees would be adequate at the cutting edge at any diameter it is the trailing edge of the primary land that may foul the workpiece if the clearance is insufficient. This is the reason for not letting the width of the primary land becoming too wide. If kept very narrow 5 degrees would be satisfactory at any diameter but this would call for frequent grinding of the secondary clearance.

Set the table at the required angle to the left side of the grinding wheel. Fit the fence, with stop screw, and set at an angle of about 1 degree with the side of the wheel. Place the end mill accessory as shown in **Photo 7,** making sure that there is clearance between cutter and wheel. Make sure all adjustments are tightened and that the cutter's edge is against the cutter rest, and then start the grinder. Using the cross feed, feed the rest until the first sparks appear.

When I first attempted to carry out this operation I started at the outer end of the end mill, sharpening towards the shank end, and found it almost impossible to feed the end mill satisfactorily. After a number of attempts, I decided to start from the shank and work towards the outer end, the difference was immense. What was beginning to look an impossible task had now become a task that could be carried out with ease. No doubt with this approach the wheel's rotation keeps the cutter against the rest and the operator needs only to make the feed.

Having successfully ground the first edge, remove the assembly from the rest, rotate the spindle counter clockwise, replace the assembly and grind the second followed by the third and fourth edges. Make sure the fence is fitted with the stop screw to ensure that the assembly returns exactly to the same position for each cutting edge. After completing the four edges, inspect the result and, if considered appropriate, repeat the procedure taking another light cut to each cutting edge, no more than 0.001", probably less.

If this results in a ground width of greater than 0.06" set the angle to 70 degrees and grind the secondary clearance to reduce the land to no more than 0.04". This operation is normally only applicable on larger size cutters, say ⁵⁄₁₆" and above.

For me, having started the exercise with what seemed insurmountable problems, the

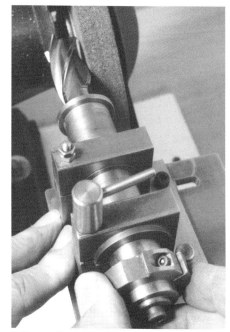

8 Sharpening taking place.

quality of the finished task was extremely satisfying. While not appearing up to the standard of a new cutter the difference was not that great. In terms of cutting ability the difference would be hard to tell.

The settings for this operation are though more critical than most, typically, if the cutter is set as **SK4**, rather than **SK5** the angle to the side of the wheel will not provide a clearance on the cutting edges and the cutter will not cut. With the cutter set as per **SK4** the angle would need increasing, the amount though would be difficult to determine and the resulting clearance would be uncertain.

The assembly is held firmly against the fence, stop screw and the surface of the rest's table using the left hand and the spindle fed by the right hand, **Photo 8.** As both hands are well away from the grinding wheel it is with normal care a safe operation. It is probably worth commenting at this point that for simplicity of taking the photographs the hands are not shown in most of the illustrations throughout the book. Manual intervention will of course be needed for the sharpening operation to be completed.

This is without doubt the most complex sharpening operation proposed in the book but creating a cutter, virtually the equal of a new one, is very satisfying and well worth the effort of making the accessory. It should not be assumed that using a full function tool and cutter grinder will make the task any quicker or easier, in fact the versatility of these may make many operations even more demanding.

SHARPENING SLOT DRILLS

Having described the operations necessary for sharpening an end mill it would be easy to fall into the trap of considering a slot drill just an end mill but with only two cutting edges, this is not the case. The most obvious difference is due to the need for a slot drill to be able to be plunged into the workpiece, a task that an end mill cannot do due to it not being able to cut completely to its center. Examination of a slot drill will show that one cutting edge is longer than the other enabling it to drill a hole. **Photo 9.**

Considering first, sharpening the end teeth and how this will differ from the process used for an end mill. The following description is based on the method used for end mills in square holders and plunged into the wheel face. Using this method and sharpening first the shorter edge, then rotating the cutter 180

degrees and grinding the second, will result in the second edge not being sharpened completely along its length. However, if the longer edge is ground first and then the cutter rotated to grind the other, the wheel would foul the innermost part of the longer edge already ground.

It would therefore seem necessary to grind one edge and then reset the assembly for grinding the other. While theoretically possible it would be difficult to get both edges at the same level and one edge would then do all or most of the work when plunging. My method for overcoming this is as follows.

First, grind the short edge and then the longer edge at the same setting, as done for an end mill, that is, creating a concave end with the fence set at 1 to 2 degrees. Now increase this angle to around 3 degrees and set the fence over so as to grind the inner portion of the longer edge. Before grinding move the infeed out a little, then adjust the infeed little by little until that part of the longer edge initially missed is ground. This will result in a small bend in the edge, **SK6**, but this will be of no consequence.

If the primary clearance land becomes over wide the secondary clearance will also need grinding. However, being less critical, the short edge can be ground, then the fence moved and the longer edge ground at one operation.

In the average home workshop slot drills will get less use than end mills and therefore the need for sharpening will be less. If a slot drill has been sharpened a number of times the shorter edge will reduce in length but more importantly so will the longer. This will result in the slot drill not cutting to the center. Examination of a slot drill will show that there is what appears at first sight an additional

NORMAL CUTTING EDGE LINE

END TEETH GROUND IN 3 STAGES
1 AND 2 AT THE SAME SETTING.
ANGLES SHOWN EXAGERATED FOR
CLARITY.

SK6. Slot drill end tooth form.

9 A slot drill has one long cutting edge that passes the center. This enables it to plunge into the workpiece for cutting enclosed slots.

clearance angle but at 90 degrees to the other two. This though is not a clearance facet but one to produce the cutting edge at the innermost part of each end tooth.

The process for creating this will be similar to that for grinding the secondary facet but at a steeper angle, not crucial but say around 45 degrees. What is crucial is that the fence position must be set so as to avoid the grinding wheel contacting the outer end of the cutting edge as a result removing the helix at that point.

The process for sharpening the cutting edges will be identical to that for an end mill, but sharpening these will reduce the size of the slot produced. Whether this is acceptable will depend on the use to which it is put.

CHAPTER 6
OTHER MILLING CUTTERS

Dovetail cutters

These can be sharpened much like end mills, though the side cutting edges not having a helix makes sharpening them an easier operation. The standard for cutters up to 25mm (or 1") outside diameter, those I consider most likely to surface in the home workshop, is for them to have 6 teeth. Ideally, therefore, the end mill accessory should be used with its 6 tooth index collar.

If you have decided not to equip yourself with this facility at this stage, a simple hexagonal holder, similar in principle to the square holders for end mills, should be made for the task and used as in **Photo 1** to sharpen the end teeth. The bore should be reasonably concentric with the sides of the holder, but more important, concentric with the corners. This can be achieved with ease by skimming

1 Using a hexagonal holder for sharpening a six tooth dovetail cutter. As can be seen, a higher fence is required for this set up.

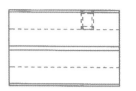

BORE TO BE CENTRAL IN HEXAGON
AND A CLOSE FIT ON THE CUTTER'S
SHANK.
SKIM CORNERS AFTER BORING TO
ENSURE THAT THEY ARE CONCENTRIC
WITH THE BORE.

SK1. Six tooth cutter holder.

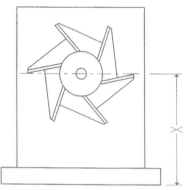

X. CUTTING TIPS PARALLEL
WITH BASE

SK2. Position for grinding outer edges.

the corners after machining the bore, doing this without removing the part from the chuck, see **SK1**. A higher fence, depending on the size of the hexagon, will be necessary for this set up.

Having six, rather than four teeth, it is probable that the grinding wheel will come close to the adjacent tooth but this can be avoided by turning the cutter in the holder a few degrees. An alternative would be to sharpen the cutter on the side of the wheel using the wheel's curvature to provide the clearance.

As with an end mill, grinding the secondary clearance will also become necessary after the cutter has been sharpened a few times. Again, the process will be the same. Both angles may differ from those given for an end mill and I would suggest you endeavour to replicate those already on the cutter.

The absence of any helix on the side cutting edges makes sharpening these an easy task

using the end mill accessory, but it is less straightforward using the simple hexagonal holder, though not impossible. Because of this I will first describe the process using the accessory.

Fit the six tooth indexing collar to the end mill accessory, ensuring that there is no end float and adjust the bearings so that the spindle rotates freely but without shake. Fit the dovetail cutter making sure that, when the index collar is located against the index arm, the tips of the opposing end teeth are horizontal, **SK2**, then lock the spindle. This can be set up on the surface plate using a surface gauge to check that the opposing tooth tips are at the same height.

Set the end mill accessory at 30 degrees on the swivel base and the rest's table at the appropriate angle to the side of the wheel then sharpen the first edge as illustrated in **Photo 2**. Remember to set the fence so that grinding only takes place on the corner of the wheel

2 Sharpening the side teeth of a dovetail cutter using the end mill accessory on the swivel base. The cutter not having a helix, this operation is relatively simple.

and set the amount removed using the cross feed. Also adjust the position of the stop screw using the infeed to prevent the cutter's shank from being ground. However, I see from the photograph that I have not heeded my advice given in an earlier chapter, that is to arrange the fence between the accessory and the wheel. I can assure you that the set up works well, with care, but one false move and the cutting edge could have more ground from it than is required. The fence should be on the hidden side of the swivel base.

Having ground the first edge, loosen the spindle, rotate to the next tooth on the index collar, lock the spindle and grind the second edge, repeating for the remaining edges. After having been sharpened a number of times the secondary clearance will also need attention in the same way, but at a steeper angle.

Photo 3 also shows that the end mill accessory can be used to sharpen the end teeth with a wiping action rather than the cruder plunge and remove illustrated in **Photo 1.**

I feel I should make a point here that is relevant, not only to this task, but also to most other sharpening tasks. Do always remove the absolute minimum, the more that you remove the sooner it will be necessary to grind other faces, most often the secondary clearance, but similarly, re-establishing the indent in the end of an end mill.

3 Sharpening the end teeth using the end mill accessory. Being done with a wiping action it is preferable to the cruder, plunge and remove method in Photo 1.

Returning now to using the simple hexagonal holder. To accomplish the task with this it will be necessary to make an angled guide, as shown in **SK3**. The guide, hexagonal holder and deeper fence are seen in **Photo 4**. To make this, fix a fence at 30 degrees to an angle plate and fix and machine the guide as illustrated in **Photo 5**.

The process is simple, just place the holder, both side and end, against the guide piece and, using a long Allen key to restrain the guide, feed the holder forward. Ensure that it stays in contact with the guide and the guide with the fence until the stop screw is reached, **Photo 6**. This may seem a crude arrangement but in fact is works quite well. Actually, a small hole in the guide to take the end of the Allen key would be a worthwhile addition.

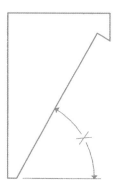

X. ANGLE TO SUIT CUTTER BEING SHARPENED. NORMALLY 45° OR 60° FOR A DOVETAIL CUTTER.

SK3. Angled guide.

4 If the end mill accessory has not been made, the parts in this photograph will enable the side teeth of a dovetail cutter to be sharpened, see Photo 6.

5 The set-up for machining the angled guide.

6 Sharpening the side teeth, this time using the hexagonal holder and the angled guide.

T SLOT CUTTERS

As can be seen in **Photo 7** the teeth of a T slot cutter have a helix, similar to that on an end mill. Closer examination though shows that this is positive and negative on alternate edges. The short length of an edge will make setting up the end mill accessory to take account of the helix very difficult, compounded by the fact that it is negative on alternate edges.

Examination of a new cutter shows that the edge is very slightly convex along its length, proving that at the manufacturing stage the helix was taken account of.

My suggestion, that I should add I have never used myself, is to sharpen the outer edges in the same manner as described for the outer edges of a dovetail cutter (see Photo 2 or 6, no guide required though). It is probable that a few extra degrees clearance will be required. This I feel will

work adequately, though, of purely academic interest only, while the edge will be straight the cut surface will be convex, due to the helix, see **SK4** for an explanation.

Apart from being small, and therefore awkward to set up, sharpening of the ends of each tooth should be possible using a similar method to that used for the end teeth of an end mill. The ends adjacent to the shank will though need particular care and probably not be possible unless a grinder with a saucer wheel is available.

The shop made cutter, right of **Photo 7**, can of course be sharpened with ease having no helix and needing only to be ground on its outer edges.

Incidentally, a T slot cutter is made oversize to allow for it to be sharpened a number of times before the resulting slot becomes too small for the T nut intended to be used in it.

SLITTING SAWS

Sketch **SK5** shows the equipment required for sharpening a slitting saw and is seen being used in **Photo 8**. The saw is fed left to right by hand with the swivel base held firmly against the fence and the saw against the swivel base. The infeed is used to control depth of cut. With a large tooth saw it is probable that no stop will be required.

However, with an accurately dressed wheel, saws with very small teeth can be ground when a stop fitted to the fence will be necessary to avoid the wheel touching the adjacent tooth. In this case the cross feed would be used to accurately set the stop position.

The pivot on which the saw rotates is drilled off center to provide adjustment, enabling differing saw diameters to locate the leaf spring used for indexing the saw. The leaf spring is also used to set the clearance angle

ground onto the saw's teeth, equal to angle Y shown on **SK5**. This can be reduced by moving the leaf spring forward and increased by moving it back.

The fence must be set at an angle of 1 to 2 degrees to the face of the wheel so that grinding only takes place on the wheel's left corner.

Details for making the parts used in this assembly are given in Chapter 11.

FLY CUTTERS AND BORING TOOLS

While essentially milling cutters, because of their similarity with lathe tools they were discussed in the final paragraph of Chapter 4.

7 Commercial and shop made T slot cutters, note the helix on the commercial item.

8 Sharpening a slitting saw.

SK4.

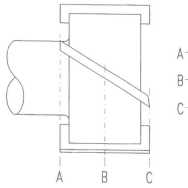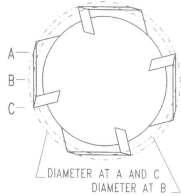

A — B — C

A B C

DIAMETER AT A AND C
DIAMETER AT B

THIS SHOWS THAT WHILST THE CUTTER HAS BEEN GROUND
WITH A STRAIGHT EDGE, AT A AND C IT CUTS AT A LARGER
DIAMETER. THE CUT FACE IS THEREFORE CONVEX. FOR EASE
THE SKETCH SHOWS ONLY FOUR CUTTING EDGES.

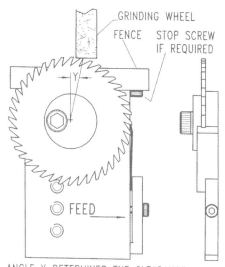

GRINDING WHEEL
FENCE   STOP SCREW
IF REQUIRED

Y

FEED

SK5. Slitting saw sharpening.

ANGLE Y DETERMINES THE CLEARANCE
ANGLE OF THE GROUND TOOTH.

CHAPTER 7
SMALL WORKSHOP TOOLS

Grinding the simpler workshop tools may appear to be a task to be carried out free hand, but, having equipped the workshop for sharpening the more complex items it would be false economy not to include accessories to grind the simpler items. In any case, some will be ground using the same accessories needed for the more complex tasks.

SCREWDRIVERS

Screwdrivers are probably ground free hand in most cases. However, if you have tried this you will have found how difficult it is to ensure the two sides are parallel. Using the round workpiece holder mounted on the swivel base, **SK1**, the task can be performed with precision, **Photo 1**. Having ground the first

1 Sharpening a screwdriver.

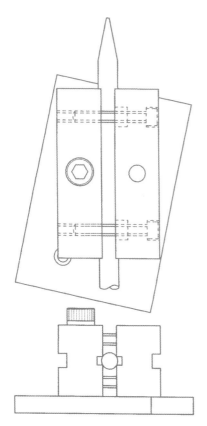

SK1. Round workpiece holder assembly.

limit the amount ground at each attempt, do not attempt to feed this totally manually.

BORING TOOLS

The subject of boring tools for boring heads, that that have round shanks, are another tool that will make use of the round workpiece holder. This subject was discussed in the final paragraph of Chapter 4.

CENTER PUNCHES

These are another item that have traditionally been sharpened free hand but a more controlled result can be accomplished, and with ease, using the end mill sharpening accessory fitted with a round workpiece holder (Chapter 11, item 81). Having only limited use, and concentricity not being crucial, this holder is simpler than making a collet to suit. Its outer diameter being made to suit one of the end mill collets. However, if you prefer you can of course make a collet to hold the center punch.

In use, the rest's fence is fitted with a stop screw and set at an angle as required by the center punch. With the accessory held against the fence and its stop the accessory's spindle is rotated while the center punch is being ground on the wheel's face, **Photo 2**. The amount ground is controlled by the rest's infeed. Take note how the ball joint of the rest permits the table to be rotated to the angle required for this operation. With a table that cannot be rotated (Photo 3, Chapter 3) the fence should be angled.

The angle of the center punch's point will depend on its intended use. Most often this will be to produce an indent for starting a drill. For this to work reliably the outer diameter of

side, the holder is removed from the base, turned over, repositioned and the second side ground.

Having ground the sides, the workpiece holder is removed from the base, then turned on its side and the end of the driver ground until the correct tip thickness results. For tasks such as this, where there is significant overhang from the holder, do ensure the holder is firmly held down on the rest's table. Also, do this using the fence with stop and infeed to

2 Sharpening a center punch.

the indent must be greater than the length of the drill's chisel point, typically around $\frac{1}{32}$" for a $\frac{5}{32}$" drill and $\frac{3}{32}$" for a $\frac{1}{2}$" drill. To produce suitable indents for the larger size drills, a relatively flat point of 90 degrees would be about right.

The center punch mark is invariably positioned on a previously scribed line but in use the 90 degree angle punch has two weaknesses. The rather flat point does not locate positively in the scribed line and being flat visibility is also limited. To overcome this problem a center punch with a sharper point is first used, often called spotting or prick punches. Punches with a point as sharp as 30 degrees are often proposed but will of course only be able to create the smallest impression due to the weakness of the point. An angle of 45 degrees to 60 degrees may be more practical for the majority of tasks.

The punched mark is then enlarged with the standard 90 degree punch prior to drilling.

In the case of an end mill accessory not being available the following method, though crude, works quite well. Push a circlip washer firmly onto the taper portion of the center punch and with a vee block located against the fence and its stop screw place the punch into the Vee with the circlip against the block's face and rotate the punch. Use the infeed to determine the amount ground off. See **SK2** and **Photo 3**.

If the punch is held in the vee block using the finger, the knurl will make rotation a little difficult. Adding a short length of round bar between the finger and the punch overcomes this problem. Also, for added security, a second circlip can be positioned against the first.

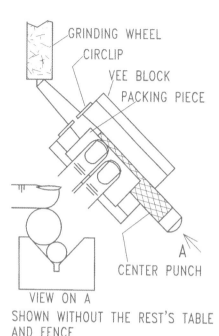

GRINDING WHEEL
CIRCLIP
VEE BLOCK
PACKING PIECE

A

CENTER PUNCH

VIEW ON A
SHOWN WITHOUT THE REST'S TABLE
AND FENCE

SK2. Sharpening a center punch.

Photo 4 shows how well a screw driver and a center punch can be ground using these technique's, far better than could be achieved by free hand methods.

SCRAPERS

Photo 5 shows 3 commercially available scrapers, though many workshop owners make their own from old files. The flat scraper, that in the center, is the one most likely to get used, while the others are normally used, in my workshop at least, for de-burring holes, round and rectangular. A more demanding task for these that crops up occasionally is to open up the bore of a bearing surface very slightly to improve fit.

The flat scraper, being used predominantly to create flat surfaces to a high degrees of accuracy, are called upon to remove metal at minimal depths of cut. Because of this the cutting edge must be very keen. It should be obvious that a cutter cannot be called upon to remove metal to a depth of say 0.0001" if

3 Sharpening a center punch using a vee block and a circlip.

4 The methods in photographs 1 and 2 produce excellent results as can be seen in this photograph.

5 Set of scrapers, the flat one in the middle, being used to produce flat surfaces, requires a very fine edge.

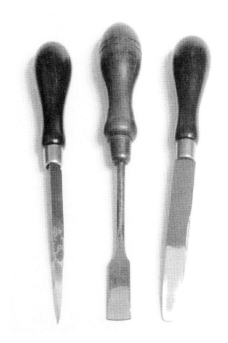

it has a cutting edge with a radius of 0.0001", it will just slide over. The scraper's edge must therefore be near perfect!

Sharpening these is a job for the flat stones. However, if the working end is in particularly poor condition then this can be initially very lightly ground to give a slightly curved end. This is one task that can be done free hand on the basic off hand grinder. Next, the end should be polished on a fine flat stone using an action as illustrated by **SK3A**. This needs to be carried out on a fairly hard stone as the narrow end will only cut a grove in it. Because of this a Japanese water stone is definitely out.

With the end now polished the two sides should be polished first using a relatively coarse stone finishing on one of say 1000 grit minimum, **SK3B**. For this a water stone would be ideal, do thoroughly clean the scraper so as to avoid contaminating the water stone. You could now put a finishing touch to the end of

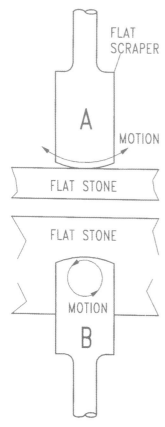

SK3. Flat scraper sharpening.

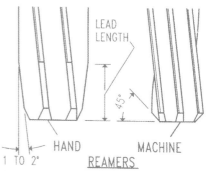

SK4. Reamer lead angles.

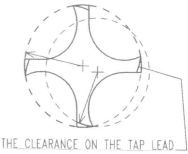

THE CLEARANCE ON THE TAP LEAD

THE CLEARANCE IS GROUND ABOUT
A DIFFERENT CENTER TO THAT OF
THE TAP ITSELF.

SK5.

the scraper on the water stone but do this away from the center of the stone so as not to damage the area most used.

REAMERS

The need to sharpen these in the home workshop should be a rarity but might surface if well used second hand reamers in the larger sizes are purchased. These are often on offer at exhibitions so it is not that unlikely. However, being intended for producing precision holes, much more so

than with a drill, sharpening them is only practical using a tool and cutter grinder. This will either be a Quorn, a Stent or a commercially available machine.

Two types of reamers are commonly available, Hand and Machine. The Hand reamer has a gradual taper of 1 to 2 degrees to enable it to start easily while the Machine reamer has a 45 degree bevel, see **SK4**. As the reamer only cuts on these edges these are the only parts of a reamer that need sharpening. Even so, this needs to be carried out very accurately and mounting the reamer between centers is the only practical method.

The radial clearance on the taper of a Hand reamer depends on its diameter and being less at the larger diameters. As a guide, say 25 degrees at ⅛" diameter and 5 degrees at ½" and above. While accuracy of the cutting edge is essential the clearance angle is not that crucial, for intermediate diameters it will be sufficient to interpolate from the above values.

The reason for the clearance angle changing with diameter is that at smaller diameters the trailing edge of the land will foul in the hole being cut, in the same way as a boring tool for the lathe is more critical at smaller bore diameters. If the land could be kept very small by the use of secondary clearance, 5 degrees could be used at any diameter.

The length of the taper lead on a Hand reamer should typically be 1 to ½ times the reamer's diameter, but with a maximum length of ¾" for larger sizes. However, replicating what already exists would be a good starting point. In the case of a Machine reamer the clearance on the bevel should be in the order of 5 to 10 degrees.

TAPS

Like reamers, the need to sharpen taps in the home workshop will be an infrequent requirement at which time purchasing a new tap will no doubt be the way forward for most workshop owners.

Not achieving a constant lead length when sharpening a tap will result in oversize threads being produced so accuracy is vital. Again this points to the need for a tool and cutter grinder. If you look at a new taper tap in a larger size you will see that the clearance behind the cutting edge has a curved surface indicating that it was not rotated about its center whist being ground, see **SK5**. This would seem right outside the limits of what is practical for almost all home workshops.

Even so, it would be worthwhile producing a flat clearance as would be done with the outer cutting edges of an end mill should it be essential to recondition an existing tap. The task would still need carrying out between centers but worth attempting if you have the machinery to do it and a tap costing sufficient to warrant the effort. I have no experience in sharpening a tap with a flat clearance but see no reason why it should not produce reasonably satisfactory results.

Not having a tool and cutter grinder I am unable to take photographs of taps and reamers being sharpened, but then this book is aimed at using simper methods. I suspect that many that do own such machines do not get the maximum benefit from having them and would urge owners to acquire more detailed reading on their use. There is a book on using the Quorn, also, books aimed at the industrial user that would be worth studying.

CHAPTER 8
WOODWORKING TOOLS

Unlike metalworking, where much of the activity is mechanized , woodworking for the occasional woodworker is very much a manual activity. For this reason keeping your woodworking tools perfectly sharp is essential else the task will become laborious. A major difference between woodworking tools and metalworking tools is the angle at the cutting edge, metalworking, say 70 to 85 degrees while woodworking tools are typically 30 degrees. Even though the edges of both are sharpened to a perfect edge the much smaller angle enables woodworking tools to be razor sharp.

The tooling used for sharpening them is also different as the cutting edge is created manually on a flat stone, only an off hand grinder, or similar, being used initially to create an edge prior to sharpening, typically when a plane blade has become damaged. However, in this situation, considerable care must be exercised as overheating of the cutting edge can so easily result due to the limited mass of metal at the edge to absorb the heat generated.

Some frequently used woodworking tools while able to be sharpened in the home

workshop are best left to the professional, for me handsaws fit into this category. Having over a number of years attempted to sharpen handsaws myself, I eventually sent them to the local saw doctor. The difference being so marked that I have now decided that this is the best course of action as it is not overly expensive; no doubt these days it is an automated process.

Should you have a mechanized planner then this is also an item best left to a commercial operation, unless of course you have a Stent, or some other surface grinder.

SHARPENING EQUIPMENT

Where practical to sharpen woodworking tools in the home workshop the equipment required is relatively inexpensive. Your normal off hand grinder will suffice for re establishing new edges for sharpening if they become damaged. There are though variations that are specifically intended for using with woodworking tools and therefore have advantages. The simplest variation is for one of the wheels to be wider than the norm at around 1½". This makes it easier to

1 A wet stone grinder, the large wheel runs in a bath of water and runs at a much lower speed.

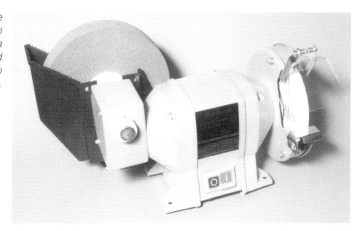

recondition wider tools with the wheel grade also more appropriate for the task.

Even better for the task is a grinder having a larger wheel, both diameter and width, but geared to run at a much lower speed. These may also have a smaller wheel running at the usual 3450 RPM, **Photo 1** is an example. The grade of the large wheel is again chosen for the task and runs in bath of water, helping to keep the wheel clean and the tool being ground cool.

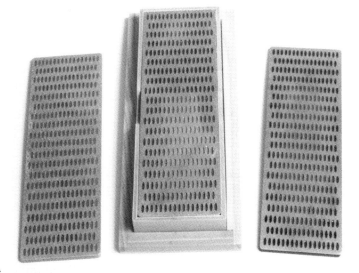

2 Diamond flat stones.

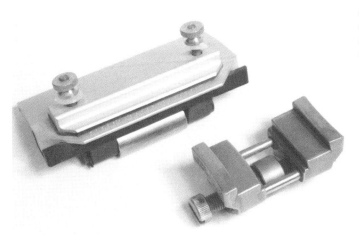

3 Honing guides used mainly for chisels and plane blades, see Photo 5.

FLAT STONES

These come in a multitude of materials and shapes. The relatively coarse aluminum oxide flat stones are only appropriate for the initial repair of slightly damaged edges. A much finer stone is essential for achieving a razor sharp edge and 1000 grit should be considered a minimum.

For even finer edges and polished surfaces flat stones are available up to 10,000 grit, maybe more. There is a range of types available; including some made from industrial diamonds and with some known as water stones that are stored in water between uses. Unless you are involved in a large amount of woodwork the actual choice is not that important, all will give a reasonable result.

In use, some flat stones will become concave and make accurate sharpening difficult. This effect will be almost zero in the case of both diamond, **Photo 2**, and sapphire stones, though their make up is quite different. Both are comparatively expensive.

More traditional flat stones are aluminum oxide and Japanese water stones. Aluminum oxide stones are predominantly made at the coarser end of the spectrum with water stones fine to very fine. These stones are much more prone to wear with the water stones being particularly so. However, the water stones are relatively easy to flatten as they use a softer bond material.

To flatten a stone, place a sheet of wet and dry sandpaper, say 60 to 100 grit, on a flat surface and lap the stone on this until a flat surface results.

These comments regarding flat stones are very much abbreviated as there are many variations in material make up and modern production methods are reducing the cost of diamond and sapphire stones, making them more affordable. It is a measure of the types of materials used and their varying make up that the catalogs of suppliers to the home workshop have a lot of technical data regarding the various types. This is particularly so for those suppliers that supply to the woodworker.

HONING GUIDES AND RESTS

Sharpening tools free hand is far from impossible but honing guides, being

4 Two commercial grinding rests suitable for sharpening woodworking tools.

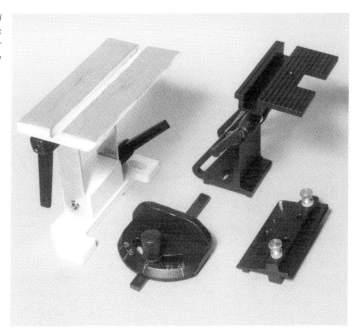

inexpensive, are certainly worth considering as they will enable a consistent result to be achieved, **Photo 3** shows two typical examples.

As mentioned in Chapter 1, the tool rests fitted to off hand grinders are totally inadequate, even for woodworking tools, and additional facilities need to be provided. This can be a commercially available item; **Photo 4** show's two, or a shop made item such as that detailed in Chapter 9. Actually, the commercial rests, while inadequate for the metalworking workshop, are quite satisfactory for woodworking tools.

CHISELS

Armed with your chisel and a mallet it is easy to fall into the trap of thinking that the chisel is a brute force instrument. This is far from the truth and much of the more detailed

work is done with no more than using arm pressure. My comment above about keeping your tools sharp is therefore very relevant here.

Most workshops will be equipped with tools that have been used for many years. However, if you purchase new items the first thing that becomes obvious is that they are in need of sharpening, only the secondary face having been ground. Creating the primary angle is only part of the task.

The first task is to flatten the back of the blade then bring it to a near mirror finish. The professional cabinet maker will use a metal lapping plate with lapping paste for the flattening process but while these are used in the metalworking workshop they are not that common. Because of that, a good compromise is to use wet and dry abrasive paper on a small piece of plate glass or some

5 Final sharpening of a chisel on a water stone. Note the container of water in the background for washing and storing the water stone.

other surface plate. Start with about 120 grit and working up to say 600 grit, aim to get an even gray finish over at least 2" of the blade at the working end.

Wipe the blade clean so as to not contaminate your fine flat stones and polish the rear, working up to the finest stone you have, hopefully at least 6000 grit. Having done this once there should not be a need to do this again if the chisels are taken care of. If you have chisels which are old, or never having been flattened and polished, then it is never too late.

With the rear polished the next stage is to sharpen the cutting edge. Using a honing guide, set at 30°, polish the cutting bevel first with a 1000 grit stone and finally with a 6000 grit, **Photo 5**. A very fine burr will result on the cutting edge, remove this by very lightly honing the rear of the blade until the burr falls away. The result should be a razor sharp edge.

If you do not have a stone as fine as 6000 grit, use the finest that you have. However, if this is quite coarse, then now is the time make a purchase, a double sided Japanese water stone, 1000/ 6000 grit would not be over expensive.

The photograph shows that the water stone is placed in a tin lid to protect the bench from the wet stone and that this is clamped to the bench to prevent it moving. In the background is a container of water in which the stone is washed periodically during the sharpening operation and stored after use. Ideally the container should have an airtight lid to prevent evaporation, else you will find the stone dry and not ready for use next time a tool needs sharpening.

When the primary bevel land becomes too wide, say over ¹⁄₁₆", the secondary bevel, 25 degrees, will require attention to reduce this width. Having a greater surface area than the primary bevel it is impractical to do this

6 Using the Wet stone grinder with one of the commercial rests to produce the secondary angle on a chisel.

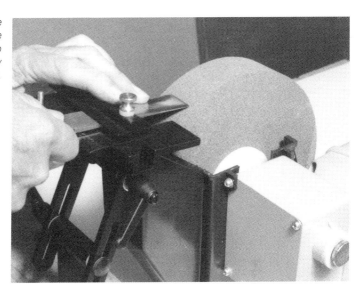

on the flat stone, as the task would be very time consuming. This therefore is a job for the bench grinder, **Photo 6** shows the task being undertaken on the grinder with a wet stone. Note how the chisel is held at 90° to the wheel in a holder that then slides along a grove in the rest, creating a straight edge as a result.

Having arrived at your razor sharp chisel, do use and store it with care. If not provided with the chisel when purchased, do make a cap of some form to protect the cutting edge while not in use.

PLANE BLADES

The process for sharpening these follows very closely that for sharpening a chisel including polishing the rear of the blade. There is though one possible exception. Some cabinet makers recommend that the cutting edge of the blade should be very slightly curved so that it cuts only on about the center 1⅛" to 1⅜" of the blade's width. This prevents the

blade making noticeable steps when planning wide boards. The curve is produced by very slightly rocking the blade to one side and the other when polishing the primary bevel.

If purchasing a new plane, or an older one that has not been properly set up, it will be necessary to flatten the base of the plane. Without carrying this out you cannot expect to produce accurate work, or take very fine finishing cuts, if the base of the plane is either bowed or twisted. This is likely to be the case unless you purchase one of the top quality planes, such as a Clifton or a Lie-Nielsen. These though will be outside most people's budget. To flatten the base fasten a sheet of 60 grit wet and dry to a sheet of plate glass, or some other flat surface and work the base of the plane over this until it becomes uniformly gray in appearance. However, this appearance may result if the base is bowed, do therefore also check with a straight edge. Finally, using the same set up, give the base a

polish using a finer sheet of wet and dry, say 600 grit or finer.

It is also essential that the edge of the cap iron that clamps directly to the face of the blade is perfectly flat. Again, lapping this on a sheet of wet and dry will be the method to use. This action will ensure that shavings do not become trapped under it and prevent the plane working effectively. While by no means should the cap iron have a razor sharp end, a fine edge will also be beneficial in this respect.

DRILL BITS

There are many types of drills used for woodworking, often not that easy to sharpen. There are though two types commonly available that are reasonably easy to grind. These are the Lip and Spur bits and the Flat bits, **Photo 7**. As hole sizes in wood are rarely that critical, precision is not called for when sharpening these and other types of drills.

Many of the economy drill grinding accessories, such as those used with a pistol drill, provide facilities for grinding these types of drills. **Photo 8** shows a Lip and Spur drill being ground on such a jig. Flat bits can also be ground but in both cases the individual cutting edges are ground without any stop mechanism. It is therefore totally in the hands of the operator to ensure both sides are sharpened equally. The central point is not ground.

Most, if not all, of these sharpening aids are equipped with a green grit wheel enabling tungsten masonry drills to be sharpened. If you do contemplate acquiring one of these sharpening aids you should know that there are a few that use similar techniques, but are self contained with their own drive motor. These also have facilities for sharpening chisels, plane blades, etc., though not to the standard required for serious woodworking, more a DIY aid.

Photo 9 shows how a flat bit can be ground while held in the round workpiece holder, just turning the assembly over for sharpening the second edge. The edge is sharpened with a plunge and remove action, but using the

8 Sharpening a lip and spur drill on a pistol drill sharpener attachment.

9 Sharpening a flat bit using the round workpiece holder to position the bit.

end stop on the fence to ensure both edges are sharpened at the same level avoids the guesswork inherent in the DIY set-up.

Another point worth taking note of is that the fence is set to create the required angle on the end of the bit and not the more usual 1 to 2 degrees where the item being ground skirt's the corner of the wheel.

The same set-up will be suitable for lip and spur drills.

SCRAPERS

Sharpening woodworking scrapers is without doubt quite unlike any other sharpening operation and probably one that will come as a surprise to the uninitiated. **Photo 10** shows a set of scrapers and both commercial and makeshift burnishers. Considering a straight edge scraper used for finishing large flat surfaces, a tabletop typically, the scraper

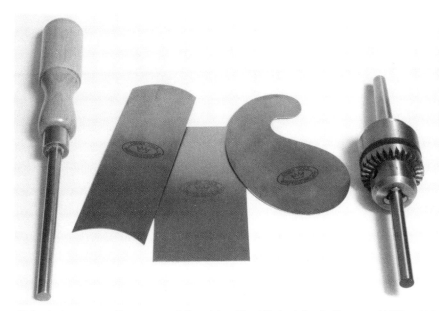

10 A set of scrapers with a commercial burnisher. The drill chuck fitted with a round HSS tool bit makes is an alternative to the commercial burnisher on the left.

should take very thin shavings rather like a plane set very fine; for this to be possible the scraper must have a razor sharp edge. This is unlike a scraper used for metalworking that has a cutting edge of virtually 90 degrees.

Assuming that the scraper edge is in poor condition the two long edges should be filed, or ground, and then honed to give a straight edge and at 90 degrees to the faces. If the scraper only needs its edge sharpening then this operation may be bypassed sometimes. The photograph shows on the left a burnisher that is used to create the cutting edge. Also shown is a drill chuck with shank and fitted with a piece of round high-speed steel, this will be a reasonable alternative for occasional use.

First, lay the scraper on the bench edge and move the burnisher along one edge using pressure as shown by **SK1A**. This will result in a shape shown in **SK1B**. Then, with the scraper held in the bench vise the edge is again flattened as illustrated by **SK1C** resulting in the shape shown in **SK1D**. Finally the burnisher is angled, **SK1E**, so as to produce what is termed a hook, **SK1F**. For clarity the resulting shapes are shown exaggerated. In use a scraper sharpened in this way will generate a surface ready for final finishing with a fine emery paper, say 400 grit. Having completed the first edge the other three edges can be sharpened similarly, **SK1G**.

The same basic process will be used for scrapers having curved edges but will of course be somewhat more difficult to perform.

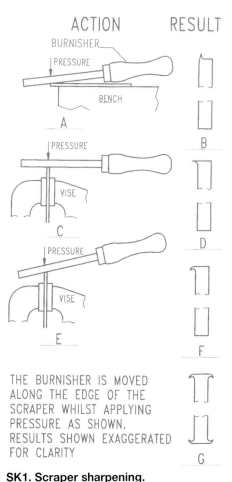

ACTION   RESULT

BURNISHER

PRESSURE

BENCH

A

PRESSURE

B

VISE

C

PRESSURE

D

VISE

E

F

THE BURNISHER IS MOVED
ALONG THE EDGE OF THE
SCRAPER WHILST APPLYING
PRESSURE AS SHOWN.
RESULTS SHOWN EXAGGERATED
FOR CLARITY

G

SK1. Scraper sharpening.

OTHER TOOLS

Chisels, planes and scrapers are the most likely to require sharpening and are by far the most demanding in terms of keeping a keen edge. Other items, some drill bits typically, seem to go on working forever. This is probably due in part to limited usage rather than staying power. Even so, such tools will occasionally benefit from attention.

There is though an advantage with many woodworking tools, that is the tool is not fully hard. Most will be aware that saws can be sharpened with a triangular file, though this is not so with the modern hard point variety.

For other tools, applying a file to some unimportant part of the cutters can easily test this. Hole cutting tools such as Auger Bits, Forstner and Saw tooth Cutters will often be found to be relatively soft. In this case improved performance can be achieved by application of a fine file to the appropriate cutting edges even if it does not fully match the capability of a new cutter.

Observe the existing angles and try to replicate these when sharpening them using a suitably shaped fine file. **Photo 11** shows a Forstner saw tooth cutter being sharpened in this way.

While I have said that it is not worth the effort to sharpen a hand saw, large pitch jigsaw blades can be given a new lease of life using a suitable file while replicating the existing cutting angles.

Router bits are through hard and their complex shapes would appear to make them a non starter for sharpening. Fortunately, the inner face is flat and can easily be honed to improve the cutting edge using a diamond file as seen in **Photo 12**. As routers run at a very high speed it is essential to keep cutters in good condition or burning of the wood will result. Fortunately, the tungsten cutting edge will not be affected by the heat, which is why it will keep working, even if poorly.

11 Many woodworking tools are not fully hard and can be sharpened using a hand file.

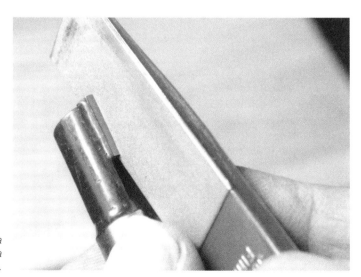

12 Sharpening a router bit with a small diamond file.

CHAPTER 9
MAKING A GRINDING REST

The remaining chapters provide the designs for most of the accessories seen being used in the book. Contrary to my usual approach I am not including extensive manufacturing details as the processes are mostly quite simple, but if you would like help in this direction, many of the items appear in the book "Milling for Home Machinists." I am though including photographs of a few of the more complex manufacturing set ups.

As the material was originally conceived and written for the UK market, the drawings are, naturally, represented in metric units. A quick study of the design, however, will show that slight variations in thickness of most of the components will not affect function and imperial sized stock may easily be substituted. In the case of fasteners, there is room for adjustment as well. Simply pick a close sized imperial fastener and adjust the tap hole and

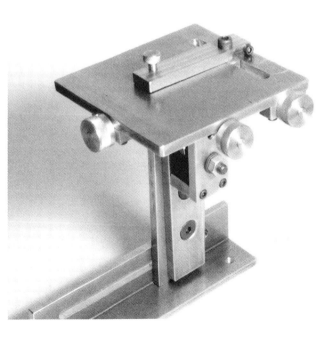

1. The completed rest.

2 This photograph of the finished parts shows that they are all easy items to make.

clearance hole sizes accordingly. For instance, an M6 screw (6mm, or .236" diameter) can easily be replaced with a ¼" screw.

The conversion of metric dimensions to imperial will result in numbers that don't match the usual fractional divisions of an inch, but since a machinist's measuring equipment and machines are set up to work in decimal divisions (thousandths of an inch), the conversion should pose no problems. Just remember, one inch equals 25.4 millimeters, so to convert the drawing dimensions divide by 25.4, or if you prefer, multiply by 0.03937.

A SIMPLE GRINDING REST

While not having the capabilities of a tool and cutter grinder, this basic rest, together with the appropriate accessories, will give perfectly adequate results for virtually all sharpening requirements in the average home workshop.

COMMON DESIGN FEATURE

A common feature on many grinding rests is the method of adjusting the angle and distance to the wheel, invariably consisting of a link, or links, pivoted at both the base and the rest's table. While this works well, in use it is more demanding to set up than would first appear to be the case. Primarily, the lower pivot adjusts the distance to the wheel and the upper pivot the angle. However, each will have an effect on the setting of the other.

PROBLEM OVERCOME

The method adopted by this rest to overcome this situation is to make the method of setting the distance to the wheel linear rather than angular. This should be obvious from **Photo 1**. Compare this with Photo 4, Chapter 8 that shows two basic rests available commercially.

MANUFACTURE

While there are quite a number of parts that make up this rest, it can be seen from **Photo 2** that they are all relatively simple. For the lathe-only workshop this will be of particular value as it is well within the capabilities of such a workshop.

It will be necessary before you commence work on the item to decide whether the height of the rest as drawn will suit the grinder with which it is to be used. In my case it is being used with a 150mm grinder having its spindle 170mm above the mounting surface. If being used at an appreciably different height, the Height adjuster (14) and the Vertical bar (15) may need their lengths changed.

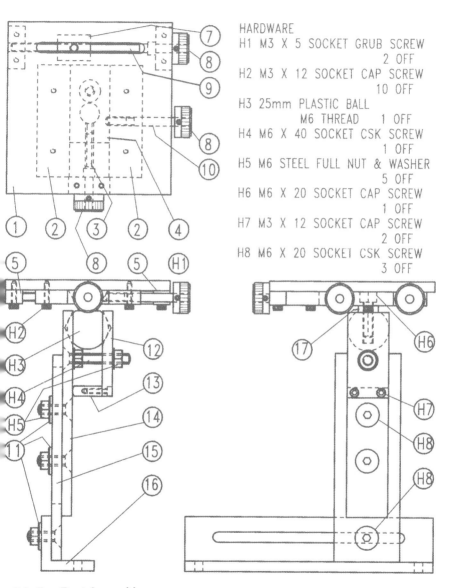

HARDWARE
H1 M3 X 5 SOCKET GRUB SCREW
2 OFF
H2 M3 X 12 SOCKET CAP SCREW
10 OFF
H3 25mm PLASTIC BALL
M6 THREAD   1 OFF
H4 M6 X 40 SOCKET CSK SCREW
1 OFF
H5 M6 STEEL FULL NUT & WASHER
5 OFF
H6 M6 X 20 SOCKET CAP SCREW
1 OFF
H7 M3 X 12 SOCKET CAP SCREW
2 OFF
H8 M6 X 20 SOCKET CSK SCREW
3 OFF

Grinding Rest Assembly

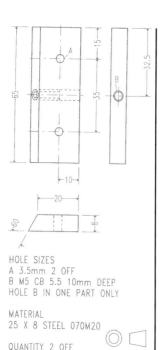

HOLE SIZES
A 3.5mm 2 OFF
B M5 CB 5.5 10mm DEEP
HOLE B IN ONE PART ONLY

MATERIAL
25 X 8 STEEL 070M20

QUANTITY 2 OFF

2. Outer dovetails.

HOLE SIZES
A 6mm CB 10mm 6.5 DEEP
B 12mm
C M5

MATERIAL
25 X 8 STEEL 070M20

QUANTITY 1 OFF

4. Inner dovetail.

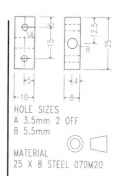

HOLE SIZES
A 3.5mm 2 OFF
B 5.5mm

MATERIAL
25 X 8 STEEL 070M20

QUANTITY 3 OFF

5. Feedscrew bearings.

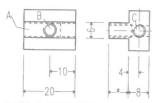

NOTE * INITIALLY 8mm FINISH
TO 6mm ON ASSEMBLY.

HOLES A 5.5mm 14mm DEEP
      B M5 9mm DEEP
      C M5

MTL. 16 SQ. STEEL 070M20

QUANTITY 1 OFF

7. Fence carrier.

3 Machining one of the dovetail faces.

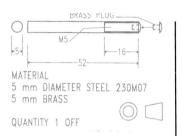

MATERIAL
5 mm DIAMETER STEEL 230M07
5 mm BRASS

QUANTITY 1 OFF

Traverse locking screw.

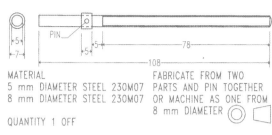

MATERIAL
5 mm DIAMETER STEEL 230M07
8 mm DIAMETER STEEL 230M07

QUANTITY 1 OFF

FABRICATE FROM TWO
PARTS AND PIN TOGETHER
OR MACHINE AS ONE FROM
8 mm DIAMETER

9. Crossfeed screw.

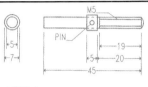

MATERIAL
5 mm DIAMETER STEEL 230M07
8 mm DIAMETER STEEL 230M07

FABRICATE FROM TWO PARTS AND
PIN TOGETHER OR MACHINE AS
ONE FROM 8 mm DIAMETER

QUANTITY 1 OFF

3. Infeed screw.

HOLE SIZES
A 5 mm   B M3

MATERIAL
20 mm DIAMETER
STEEL 230M07

QUANTITY 3 OFF

8. Knob.

THE DOVETAILS

The dovetails can easily be produced with a tilting vise (or adjustable angle plate) and an end mill, **Photo 3**, and as the complete assembly is being made in the workshop, the angle is not crucial providing the vise is not moved between machining the three parts.

In theory, the two sides of the Inner dovetail (4) need to be parallel but as the Traverse Locking Screw (10 + 8) holds it against only one of the Outer Dovetails (2), precision is not that important.

THE BALL SEATS

Both the Height Adjuster (14) and the Head Clamp (12) have countersinks in which the

4 Boring a ball seating using a boring bar and the top slide mounted at the appropriate angle.

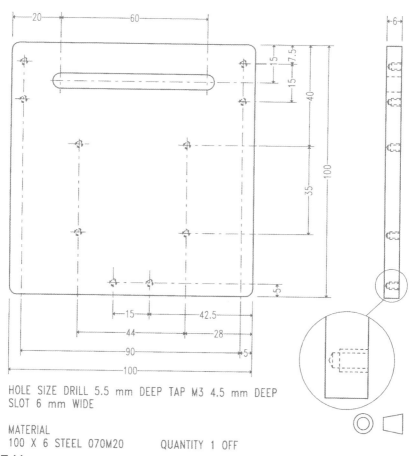

HOLE SIZE DRILL 5.5 mm DEEP TAP M3 4.5 mm DEEP
SLOT 6 mm WIDE

MATERIAL
100 X 6 STEEL 070M20   QUANTITY 1 OFF

1. Table.

25mm plastic ball (H3) sits. The countersink, being both large and not to a standard angle, will require to be machined on the lathe having the top slide set to the appropriate angle, **Photo 4**. This will require the lathe to be able to swing 115mm (4½", 9" diameter swing). If this is not possible then drill a hole, say 12mm diameter, and very generously deburr and smooth its edge. The ball can then be clamped between these, though it

will be necessary to alter the length of the Clamp spacer (13) to suit.

THE TABLE

Rather than marking out the holes required in this, you may choose, as I did, to use the mating parts as jigs for positioning the holes.

The M3 blind holes in the table being only 4.5mm deep will have to be tapped using just a plug tap. While this is not impossible it may

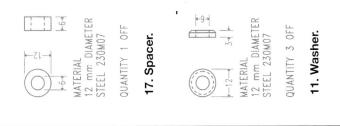

MATERIAL
12 mm DIAMETER
STEEL 230M07

QUANTITY 1 OFF

17. Spacer.

MATERIAL
12 mm DIAMETER
STEEL 230M07

QUANTITY 3 OFF

11. Washer.

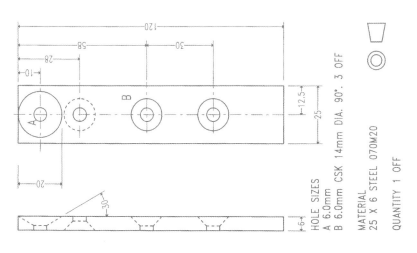

HOLE SIZES
A 6.0mm
B 6.0mm CSK 14mm DIA. 90°. 3 OFF

MATERIAL
25 X 6 STEEL 070M20

QUANTITY 1 OFF

14. Height adjuster.

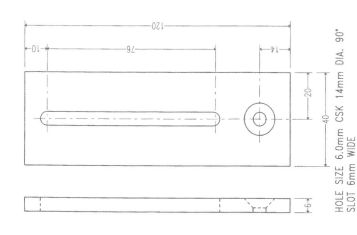

HOLE SIZE 6.0mm CSK 14mm DIA. 90°
SLOT 6mm WIDE

MATERIAL
40 X 6 STEEL 070M20

QUANTITY 1 OFF

15. Vertical bar

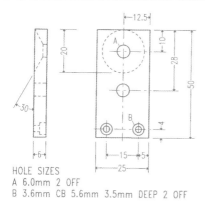

HOLE SIZES
A 6.0mm 2 OFF
B 3.6mm CB 5.6mm 3.5mm DEEP 2 OFF

MATERIAL
25 X 6 STEEL 070M20

QUANTITY 1 OFF

12. Head clamp.

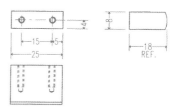

HOLES M3 X 10 DEEP 2 OFF

MATERIAL 25 X 8 STEEL 070M20

NOTE
THE 18mm DIMENSION IS A
REFERENCE VALUE. CHECK SPACING
OF ITEMS 12 AND 14 AFTER MAKING
BALL SEATINGS AND MAKE TO SUIT.

QUANTITY 1 OFF

13. Clamp spacer.

be a problem as starting with a plug tap is not easy. As a result, if the first few threads are sub standard there will not be much depth of good thread.

Unless you have a controlled feed tapping stand that will overcome this problem you may like to try the following. Take a length of steel, say 25 x 10 and around 100mm long, and tap an M3 through hole in the center. With the tap in the hole and just projecting from the other side, locate this in a hole to be tapped and clamp the bar at both ends onto the table. This will then feed the tap into the hole being tapped and should give adequate results.

To produce this very shallow thread you will need to drill the tapping hole as deep as can be done without actually breaking through and will need to set the drilling machine down feed stop to do this reliably. First, test your setting by making trial holes in a scrap piece of steel the same thickness as the table. If your tap also has a pointed end you may need to remove a little of this.

5 A view of the underside showing the working parts.

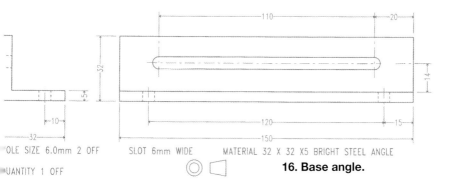

OLE SIZE 6.0mm 2 OFF SLOT 6mm WIDE MATERIAL 32 X 32 X5 BRIGHT STEEL ANGLE

QUANTITY 1 OFF

16. Base angle.

TURNING OPERATIONS

I have suggested on the drawings that the feed screws should be made from two parts that are pinned together. This will avoid turning long, slender diameters needing the use of a traveling steady. However, should you consider this preferable then make them completely from 8mm diameter.

The knobs are straightforward as drawn but you may wish to calibrate the two used with the feed screws. M5 has a pitch of 0.8mm so 40 divisions would give 0.02mm per division, a common value on metric equipment. Actually, 0.02mm is about the maximum that should be ground from a tool at one pass.

ASSEMBLY

On assembly check the spacing of items 12 and 14 and make adjustment to the 18mm dimension on the Clamp Spacer (13) as required, otherwise assembly is straightforward. Leave the slides and feedscrews dry, as any lubrication will only make removing grinding dust difficult. **Photo 5** gives a view of the underside showing the working parts.

POSSIBLE MODIFICATION

I would suggest one modification as worthwhile. To minimize the effect of any clearance between the Fence Carrier (7) and the 6mm slot in the table, I am suggesting that the carrier should be made longer as follows:

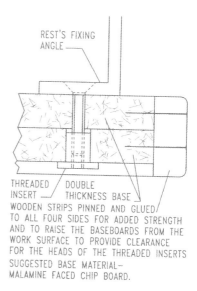

REST'S FIXING
ANGLE

THREADED / DOUBLE
INSERT / THICKNESS BASE
WOODEN STRIPS PINNED AND GLUED
TO ALL FOUR SIDES FOR ADDED STRENGTH
AND TO RAISE THE BASEBOARDS FROM THE
WORK SURFACE TO PROVIDE CLEARANCE
FOR THE HEADS OF THE THREADED INSERTS
SUGGESTED BASE MATERIAL—
MALAMINE FACED CHIP BOARD.

SK1. Rest mounting method.

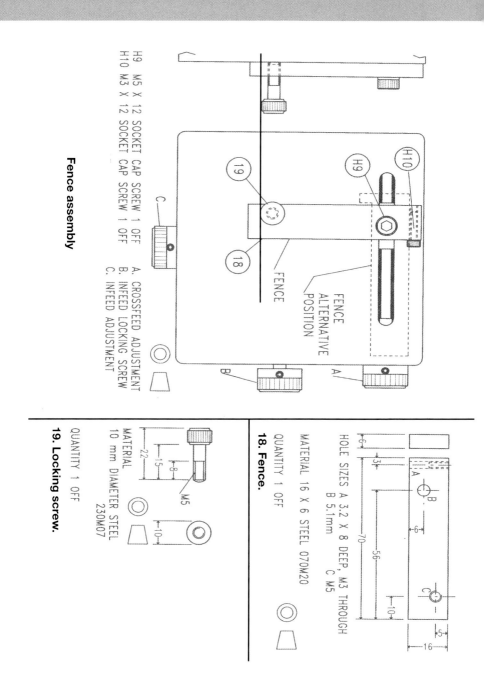

Fence assembly

H9 M5 X 12 SOCKET CAP SCREW 1 OFF
H10 M3 X 12 SOCKET CAP SCREW 1 OFF

A. CROSSFEED ADJUSTMENT
B. INFEED LOCKING SCREW
C. INFEED ADJUSTMENT

FENCE

FENCE
ALTERNATIVE
POSITION

18. Fence.

QUANTITY 1 OFF

MATERIAL 16 X 6 STEEL 070M20

HOLE SIZES A 3.2 X 8 DEEP, M3 THROUGH
B 5.1mm
C M5

19. Locking screw.

QUANTITY 1 OFF

MATERIAL
10 mm DIAMETER STEEL
230M07

M5

Make the carrier 45mm long with four M5 tapped holes at 10mm centers, rather than the single tapped hole. This will still provide 15mm fine adjustment and the fence can initially be positioned using the appropriate tapped hole from the four available.

Another minor modification worth considering is to use a countersunk screw for holding the fence to its carrier; very occasionally the accessory overlaps the swivel base and the cap head can become an obstruction. In this case temporarily fitting a short grub screw in place of the locking screw (19) may also be necessary. Similarly, an additional fixing hole in the fence can sometimes be helpful, see Photo 6 Chapter 6.

USING THE REST

Specific tasks for using the rest have been illustrated throughout the book but I would like to reiterate the following in the cause of safety. It is essential that only the fine feeds should be adjusted while the grinder is running, course adjustments only being carried out with the machine **STOPPED!**

Therefore, the angle should be set, then the coarse feeds used to locate the rest relative to the wheel, doing this while stopped. The fine feeds can then be used to set the amount to be ground away and to limit the movement in the other direction, typically to avoid the wheel touching parts not requiring to be ground, the other cutting edges of an end mill typically.

MOUNTING

Both the grinder and the rest need to be mounted on a robust base so as to avoid movement due to the forces necessary to hold the cutter in place while being ground.

A good mounting is two thicknesses of melamine faced chipboard screwed together

6 While a number of fixing positions for the rest should be provided on the base board, this arrangement will give further positions without the need for fitting additional inserts.

around their edges and with the grinder and rest fixed using screws into threaded inserts, see **SK1**. The heads on the threaded inserts will additionally hold the two boards together. The sketch also suggests that the boards be edged to both increase the strength and raise the board above the mounting bench to clear the heads of the inserts.

As the rest depends solely on the cross traverse for positioning left to right, extra mountings in the base giving alternative positions for the rest will be necessary for positioning the workpiece relative to the wheel. Even with a number of fixing positions being provided on the mounting base it is inevitable that other positions will be found advantageous in some cases. Fastening the rest to the base board using clamps, as would be used on the milling machine table, will provide for mounting the rest in other places without the need to add further fixing inserts to the base board, see **Photo 6**.

CHAPTER 10
MAKING THE END MILL SHARPENING ACCESSORY

SIMPLE ACCESSORIES

By far the simplest method of sharpening an end mill's end teeth is to use a square holder. The square can then be used to index the cutter for sharpening the four edges in turn as described in Chapter 5. Chapter 6 also describes a similar method using a hexagonal holder for cutters having 6 end teeth.

If you intend to limit the sharpening of end mills to their end teeth only, then these methods will produce acceptable results. However, I would urge you to consider eventually making the accessory in this chapter, as you will find working with fully sharp cutters much more satisfying.

THE END MILL SHARPENING ACCESSORY

This, illustrated in **AS6** and shown in **Photo 1**, is by far the most complex of the accessories in this book, enabling both end teeth and side cutting edges to be sharpened to near professional standards. It can also be used where a round workpiece needs to be rotated, typically a center punch.

Its main task though is to sharpen the edge teeth of end mills, a task that is impossible free hand or by virtually any other method. The design follows very closely that of available commercial items. However, the cost of one of these would purchase some 40 to 50 end mills so it is unlikely that one would be economic in the average home workshop.

The majority of the parts included in this fixture are simple and the following brief comments regarding the more demanding items should be sufficient.

SPINDLE

Turning the 24mm diameter parallel and concentric with the seating for the collet are the essential requirements of this part.

Mount a piece of 30mm diameter, 105mm long, in the three jaw chuck supporting the outer end with a steady, face, drill and tap M8 15mm deep. Remove, firmly fit a short hex head screw in the tapped hole, grip this in the three jaw, again supporting the outer end with a steady. Face and center drill the end, remove steady and support with the tailstock center. Turn the 24mm diameter with the flange at the tailstock end. Check before

1 The complete end mill accessory free standing.

reaching the 24mm diameter that the result is parallel, this being essential. A very small error can be eliminated by careful use of very fine emery paper.

Fit and set the fixed steady at the tailstock end on the 24mm diameter, remove the center, set the top slide to 5 degrees, make the bore, and leave the top slide at this angle for making the collets. Drill 8mm to a depth that just contacts the end of the screw. Remove from chuck and the screw from spindle and then return the spindle to chuck, now holding it on the 24mm diameter, suitably protected. Drill through 8.2mm.

COLLETS

Concentricity of the bore with the 18mm diameter and the taper is essential. To achieve this, the outer diameters and bore must be made without removing the part from the lathe. To avoid having a short stub of material left after making each collet you could consider the following that will result in no waste.

Mount a long length of material in the chuck and support with a fixed steady, doing this to allow a single collet length to project beyond the steady. After having made and parted off

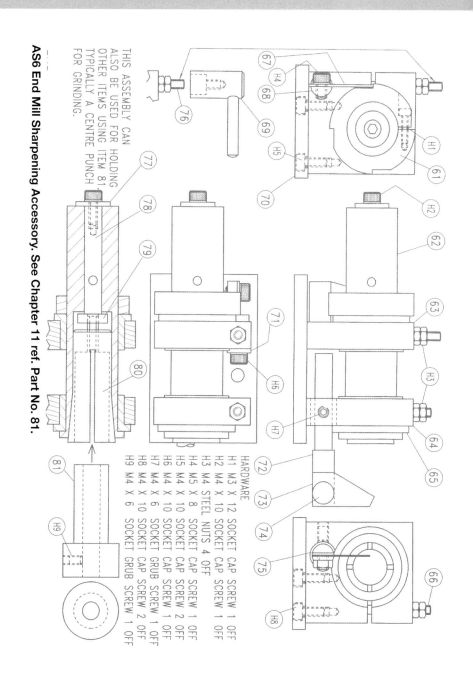

AS6 End Mill Sharpening Accessory. See Chapter 11 ref. Part No. 81.

THIS ASSEMBLY CAN
ALSO BE USED FOR HOLDING
OTHER ITEMS USING ITEM 81
TYPICALLY A CENTRE PUNCH
FOR GRINDING.

HARDWARE
H1 M3 X 12 SOCKET CAP SCREW 1 OFF
H2 M4 X 10 SOCKET CAP SCREW 1 OFF
H3 M4   STEEL NUTS 4 OFF
H4 M5 X 8   SOCKET CAP SCREW 1 OFF
H5 M4 X 10 SOCKET CAP SCREW 2 OFF
H6 M4 X 10 SOCKET CAP SCREW 1 OFF
H7 M4 X 6   SOCKET CAP SCREW 1 OFF
H8 M4 X 6   SOCKET GRUB SCREW 1 OFF
H9 M4 X 6   SOCKET GRUB SCREW 1 OFF

the first collet, move the steady sufficient for making the second collet and so on for collets three and four.

BEARINGS

Take a piece of 40mm diameter cast iron, 38mm long, and mount in the lathe chuck, drill through, say 12 to 16mm, and bore 24mm diameter 18mm deep; use the spindle as a gauge. Face the end, turn 30mm diameter by 13mm long; this process ensuring concentricity. Remove from the chuck, reverse, refit, and make the second bearing repeating the above sequence. Additionally, reduce the outer diameter to 36mm diameter.

If you are using the reverse jaws in the three jaw I would be hesitant to recommend parting off due to their limited length of grip. In this case remove from the lathe and saw in half, return and face sawn ends to the 16mm length.

2 Boring the bearing supports.

Aligning the bearing supports prior to machining their bases to ensure they are both the same height.

FRONT/REAR BEARING SUPPORTS

Cut two pieces of steel, surface edges, and drill and tap smaller holes. Mark out the position for the 30mm hole, drill 6mm diameter. Place a short length of 6mm rod through the two holes to align them and mount on the faceplate. Carefully advance the tailstock center into the 6mm hole to centralize it and firmly clamp parts in place. Push a length of bar through the lathe mandrel bore from the changewheel end to make the short length of rod available for removal. Balance faceplate assembly.

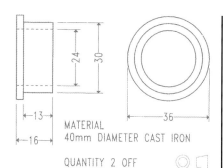

MATERIAL
40mm DIAMETER CAST IRON

QUANTITY 2 OFF

65. Bearings.

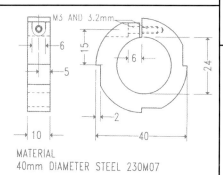

MATERIAL
40mm DIAMETER STEEL 230M07

QUANTITY 1 OFF

ADDITIONAL COLLARS MAY BE REQUIRED
FOR USE WITH CUTTERS HAVING MORE
THAN FOUR CUTTING EDGES.

61. 4-way indexing collar.

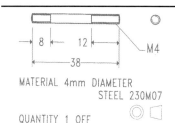

MATERIAL 4mm DIAMETER
                    STEEL 230M07

QUANTITY 1 OFF

66. Front bearing stud.

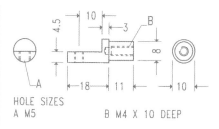

HOLE SIZES
A M5   B M4 X 10 DEEP

MATERIAL 10mm DIAMETER
                    STEEL 230M07

QUANTITY 1 OFF

68. Index arm support.

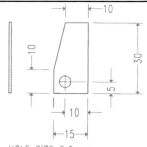

HOLE SIZE 5.2mm

MATERIAL 0.5 SHEET STEEL

QUANTITY 1 OFF

67. Index arm.

MATERIAL 4mm DIAMETER
                    STEEL 230M07

QUANTITY 1 OFF

76. Rear bearing stud.

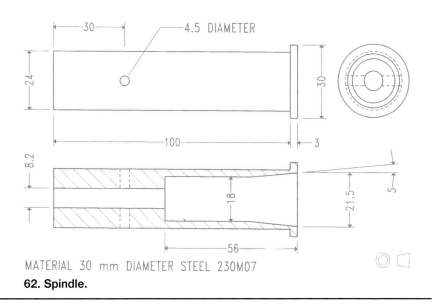

MATERIAL 30 mm DIAMETER STEEL 230M07

62. Spindle.

QUANTITY 1 OFF

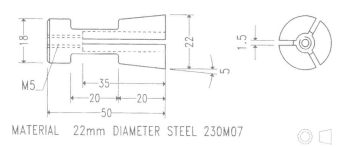

MATERIAL   22mm DIAMETER STEEL 230M07

MAKE ONE TO SUIT EACH CUTTER TO BE HELD MAKING THE
WAIST DIAMETER TO CREATE A WALL THICKNESS OF 1mm.

80. Collet.

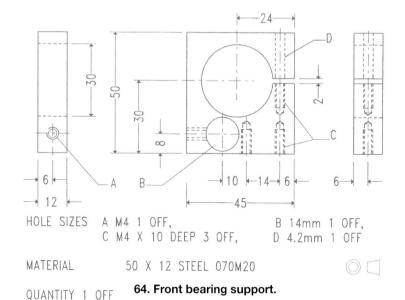

HOLE SIZES   A M4 1 OFF,   B 14mm 1 OFF,
                C M4 X 10 DEEP 3 OFF,   D 4.2mm 1 OFF

MATERIAL   50 X 12 STEEL 070M20

QUANTITY 1 OFF   **64. Front bearing support.**

HOLE SIZES   A 8mm,   B M4 X 10 DEEP 3 OFF,
                D 4.2mm 1 OFF

MATERIAL   50 X 12 STEEL 070M20

QUANTITY 1 OFF   **63. Rear bearing support.**

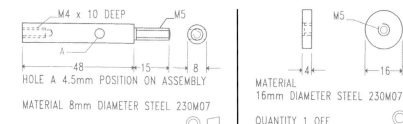

M4 x 10 DEEP   M5

A

48   15   8

HOLE A 4.5mm POSITION ON ASSEMBLY

MATERIAL 8mm DIAMETER STEEL 230M07

QUANTITIY 1 OFF

78. Collet draw bar.

M5

4   16

MATERIAL
16mm DIAMETER STEEL 230M07

QUANTITY 1 OFF

79. Collet extractor bush.

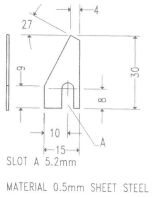

27

4

9

30

8

10

A

15

SLOT A 5.2mm

MATERIAL 0.5mm SHEET STEEL

QUANTITY 1 OFF

73. Tooth rest.

8

13

12   A   1   14

HOLE SIZE
A 4mm 2mm DEEP, POSITION ON ASSEMBLY

MATERIAL 16mm DIAMETER STEEL 230M07

QUANTITY 1 OFF

75. Tooth rest support clamp ring.

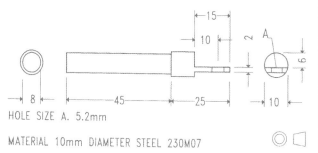

15

10   2   A

6

8   45   25   10

HOLE SIZE A. 5.2mm

MATERIAL 10mm DIAMETER STEEL 230M07

QUANTITY 1 OFF

72. Tooth rest support.

M5

7   10

1

MATERIAL
10mm DIAMETER STEEL 230M07

QUANTITY 1 OFF

74. Tooth rest screw.

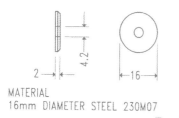

MATERIAL
16mm DIAMETER STEEL 230M07

QUANTITY 1 OFF

77. Collet closing washer.

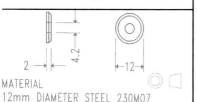

MATERIAL
12mm DIAMETER STEEL 230M07

QUANTITY 1 OFF

71. Index arm support washer.

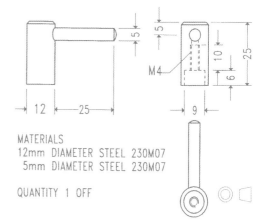

MATERIALS
12mm DIAMETER STEEL 230M07
5mm DIAMETER STEEL 230M07

QUANTITY 1 OFF

69. Spindle locking lever.

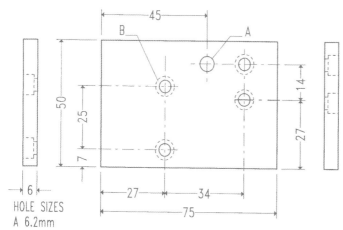

HOLE SIZES
A 6.2mm
B 4.5mm C.BORE 7.5mm DIAMETER X 4.5mm DEEP 4 OFF

MATERIAL 75mm X 6mm STEEL 070M20

70. Base. Quantity 1 off.

4 Machining the bearing support bases.

5 The rear bearing support makes the task of holding the arm support easy for machining the flat.

Bore to a diameter about 0.05mm larger than the bearing outer diameter. Fit and adjust the saddle stop to ensure the boring tool does not contact the faceplate, **Photo 2**. Fit the bearings using two part epoxy adhesive.

To ensure the spindle rotates and slides freely without shake it is essential that both bearings be at the same height and in line, the following ensures this is achieved. Mount the two bearings on an angle plate using the spindle to align the bearings. Do this with the angle plate mounted in the vise as in **Photo 3,** as this is much easier than performing the task with the angle plate surface vertical.

The fixings in the two parts must be aligned correctly when mounting the parts on the angle plate, else the bearings will not be in line when mounted to the base (70). Note that the right hand hole B in Part 63 is 15mm from the edge while the left-hand hole in Part 64 is 20mm. This means that the pitch between them must be accurately set to the difference of 5mm. With this done the bearings should easily align, with a little help from the clearance in the fixing holes. Machine the base of the bearing supports, **Photo 4**.

REMAINING PARTS

The remaining parts are all relatively simple but one point is worthy of mention and relates to machining the flat on the Index Arm Support (68). Machining the flat is of course easy but how is such a small item securely held. **Photo 5** shows how the rear bearing support (63) makes the task of holding it easy.

ASSEMBLY

This is a simple task but it may be advisable to work the spindle back and forward and rotate it in its bearings with a little lapping paste applied so as to improve fit.

CHAPTER 11
MAKING SIMPLE ACCESSORIES FOR THE GRINDING REST

The grinding rest on its own is no more than an improved rest for the off hand grinder. However, with a few simple accessories, such as those in this chapter, it can rival a tool and cutter grinder for much of the sharpening work required in the average home workshop.

SQUARE WORKPIECE HOLDER ASSEMBLY (AS3)

Photo 1. This comprises the square workpiece holder (32) and the swivel base (31). Manufacture is straightforward and needs no explanation.

1 Square Workpiece Holder Assembly.

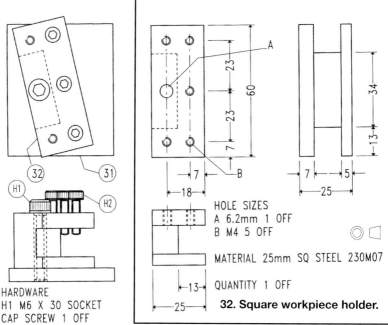

HARDWARE
H1 M6 X 30 SOCKET
CAP SCREW 1 OFF
H2 M4 X 16 SOCKET
CAP SCREW 3 OFF

AS3. Square workpiece holder assembly.

The main purpose of the holder is to hold square section lathe tools but no doubt other uses will surface. The base (31) is used for setting the angle of the workpiece relative to the feed direction and is also used with many of the other accessories.

ROUND WORKPIECE HOLDER ASSEMBLY (AS4)

Photo 2. This is also normally mounted on the swivel base, similar to using the square workpiece holder, and is used typically for holding screwdrivers, a wheel dresser and round section lathe tools, etc.

HOLE SIZES
A 6.2mm 1 OFF
B M4 5 OFF

MATERIAL 25mm SQ STEEL 230M07

QUANTITY 1 OFF

32. Square workpiece holder.

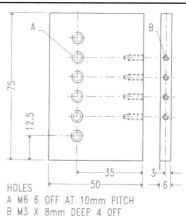

HOLES
A M6 6 OFF AT 10mm PITCH
B M3 X 8mm DEEP 4 OFF

MATERIAL 50mm X 6mm STEEL 070M20

QUANTITY 1 OFF

31. Swivel base.

AS4. Round workpiece holder assembly.

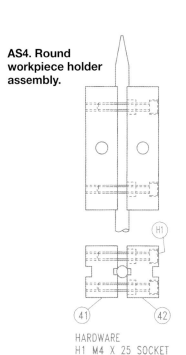

H1

HARDWARE
H1 M4 X 25 SOCKET
CAP SCREW 4 OFF

41   42

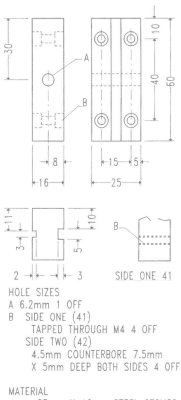

HOLE SIZES
A 6.2mm 1 OFF
B SIDE ONE (41)
      TAPPED THROUGH M4 4 OFF
   SIDE TWO (42)
      4.5mm COUNTERBORE 7.5mm
      X 5mm DEEP BOTH SIDES 4 OFF

MATERIAL
     25mm X 16mm STEEL 070M20

QUANTITY 1 OFF EACH

41, 42. Sides 1 & 2.

The main factor that must be born in mind during manufacture is that the grooves must be central, else they will not align if one part is turned over relative to the other. It is also made with dual width grooves, 3mm for items up to 6mm diameter and 5mm wide for up to 11mm diameter. The 11mm maximum is limited by the 15mm spacing of the fixing screws but a bigger version could be made for larger diameters.

2 Round Workpiece Holder Assembly.

SLITTING SAW SHARPENING ASSEMBLY (AS5)

Photo 3. Again, this uses the swivel base with a few simple parts (51, 52 and 53) added. No comments are necessary regarding making these items other than to say that the leaf spring may require bending at "X" to improve indexing on smaller tooth saws.

ROUND WORKPIECE HOLDER (81)

Photo 4. This is an alternative to using just a collet with the end mill accessory. Its purpose is for holding a round item where the time taken to make a collet cannot be justified. A typical application would be to hold a center punch while the point is being reground. In many cases precise concentricity will not be necessary, though it would be good practice to bore the through hole "A", and turn the diameter that enters the collet, without removing the part from the chuck.

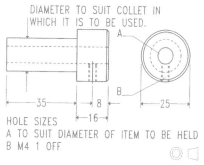

DIAMETER TO SUIT COLLET IN WHICH IT IS TO BE USED.

HOLE SIZES
A TO SUIT DIAMETER OF ITEM TO BE HELD
B M4 1 OFF

MATERIAL 25mm DIAMETER STEEL 230M07

QUANTITY 1 OFF EACH DIAMETER REQUIRED

81. Round workpiece holder.

MATERIAL SPRING STEEL 0.2mm TO 0.4mm THICK

QUANTITY 1 OFF

52. Leaf spring.

SIDE TABLE

This is fitted in place of the fence and is used for occasional off hand grinding on the side of the wheel. See chapter 4 Photo 8.

OTHER POSSIBILITIES

While the accessories I have detailed will be sufficient for the vast majority of sharpening tasks undertaken in the home workshop, specific requirements may come up that will need something different. Providing you have made yourself at home with the method of using the rest, with its fence, end stop, infeed and cross feed then designing those extras should not present a problem.

3 Slitting Saw Sharpening Assembly.

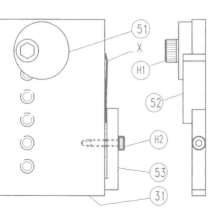

NOTE X. LEAF SPRING (52) MAY REQUIRE
BENDING TO ACHIEVE ACCURATE INDEXING
HARDWARE
1 M6 X 12 SOCKET CAP SCREW 1 OFF
2 M3 X 12 SOCKET CAP SCREW 1 OFF

AS5. Slitting saw assembly.

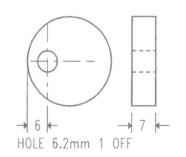

HOLE 6.2mm 1 OFF

DIAMETER TO SUIT
SLITTING SAW BORE

MATERIAL STEEL 230M07

QUANTITY 1 OFF FOR
EACH BORE SIZE

1. Slitting saw pivot.

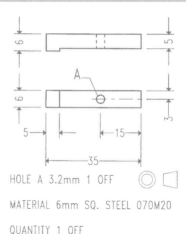

HOLE A 3.2mm 1 OFF

MATERIAL 6mm SQ. STEEL 070M20

QUANTITY 1 OFF

53. Leaf spring clamp.

HOLE 5.2mm CSK FOR M5 CSK SCREW

MATERIAL 75mm X 6mm STEEL 070M20

Side table.

4 Round Workpiece Holder.

CHAPTER 12

MAKING DRILL SHARPENING ACCESSORIES

VERY SMALL DRILLS

Very small drills, say 2mm and below, are a special case when it comes sharpening them. This is because the common drill grinding jigs available are not suitable for these sizes though I see of no reason why a scaled down version could not be made in the workshop. However, the simple jig, **Photo 1**, and shown in the drawings will sharpen these small sizes with ease. Having made and used the jig I can confirm that the drills when sharpened cut very freely. Having said that I would not like

to guarantee that the hole sizes were spot on. This will depend on the accuracy with which the diagonal vee slot is positioned and at these sizes only a very small error will produce a noticeable error in hole diameter.

Sharpening is not done on the off hand grinder but on a flat stone as seen in **Photo 2**. As a starter, align the chisel with the corner of the jig and then, looking on the non-cutting end of the drill, rotate the drill a few degrees clockwise. Position the drill with it projecting very little from the corner of the jig, say 0.004".

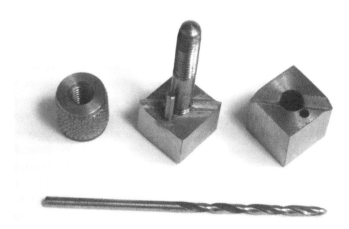

1 The parts that make up the small drill sharpening jig seen in Photo 2.

2 Using the small drill sharpening jig on a diamond flat stone.

3 Machining the vee groove. The part is held to the back plate by means of a screw into the jig's base.

With so little to remove the task is both simple and quick. You may need to experiment a little regarding the exact position of the drill in the jig to achieve the correct clearance behind the cutting edge. Clockwise rotation will increase the clearance.

MANUFACTURE

The only problem area is how to hold the parts to get both the vee slot and the raised web correctly positioned. Using the tapped holes in the two parts they can be held for machining using the set-up shown in **Photo 3.**

FOUR-FACET DRILL FORMAT

Chapter 2 included a brief description of four facet drills and their advantages and disadvantages. As was explained, sharpening

drills freehand with this form of cutting edge is all but impossible and some mechanical assistance is essential. Whatever form this takes it is essential that the drill be applied to the grinding wheel identically for both cutting edges and similarly both secondary clearance angles.

Designs have been published, in some cases using collets, others using drill chucks, that are then rotated 180degrees to enable both edges to be ground. However, any errors in the concentricity or axial alignment of the assembly will cause the second edge to be ground differently from the first. Because of this, considerable care in their manufacture will be necessary to ensure both concentricity and axial alignment is achieved.

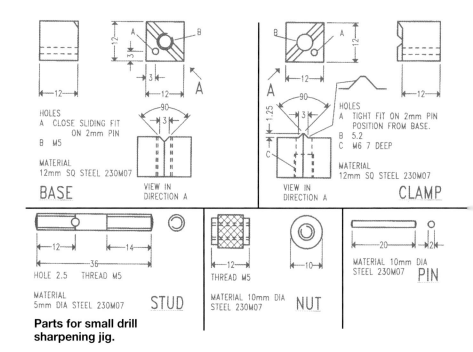

Parts for small drill sharpening jig.

Labels within the drawing:

BASE — HOLES: A CLOSE SLIDING FIT ON 2mm PIN; B M5. MATERIAL 12mm SQ STEEL 230M07. VIEW IN DIRECTION A.

CLAMP — HOLES: A TIGHT FIT ON 2mm PIN POSITION FROM BASE.; B 5.2; C M6 7 DEEP. MATERIAL 12mm SQ STEEL 230M07. VIEW IN DIRECTION A.

STUD — HOLE 2.5 THREAD M5. MATERIAL 5mm DIA STEEL 230M07.

NUT — THREAD M5. MATERIAL 10mm DIA STEEL 230M07.

PIN — MATERIAL 10mm DIA STEEL 230M07.

THE JIG

The method adopted by the jig in this chapter is to use a vee channel in which the drill rests and is rotated, a method that largely avoids the need for accuracy in its construction. Providing the drill being sharpened is not bent, and the drill is eventually rotated 180 degrees within a degree or two, perfectly acceptable results are achieved with ease.

The method of ensuring that the drill rotates 180 degrees for sharpening the second edge is by the addition of a bar that rests against the jig, first one end of the bar, then the other, resulting in the required rotation. The method is very similar to that illustrated by SK6 Chapter 2.

While the jig as drawn can only sharpen drills having the common drill point angle of 118 degrees, adapter plates could easily be made for other angles. However, as 118 degrees is by far the most common, most workshop owners will not have the need for other angles. Manufacture of the jig is very easy and really needs no detailing.

USING THE JIG

The four facet jig, seen in **Photo 4**, is used in conjunction with the grinding rest detailed in Chapter 9. It has been seen through the book that this rest in almost always mounted in front of the off hand grinder, this though is one case where mounting it at the side is a definite advantage. With the widths of the four facets being very narrow, using the curved edge of the wheel would not be a problem in terms of the sharpened drill.

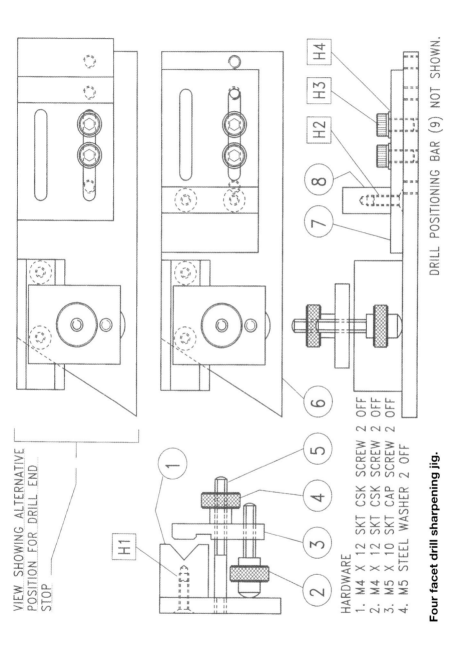

VIEW SHOWING ALTERNATIVE POSITION FOR DRILL END STOP

DRILL POSITIONING BAR (9) NOT SHOWN.

HARDWARE
1. M4 X 12 SKT CSK SCREW 2 OFF
2. M4 X 12 SKT CSK SCREW 2 OFF
3. M5 X 10 SKT CAP SCREW 2 OFF
4. M5 STEEL WASHER 2 OFF

Four facet drill sharpening jig.

However, as the height of the drill above the rest's table will vary with the drill's diameter (it resting in a vee support) then the angle would have to be set individually for each drill being sharpened. This would not be ideal if a number of drills are to be sharpened at the same time. Using the side of the wheel avoids this situation.

With the rest at the side it can be either tilted down towards the wheel or, alternatively, up. The later will require the drill to project farther from the vee mounting block, so tilting it down is preferable as the shorter projection will more precisely position the drill. Also, in this position the weight of the jig will assist in keeping it against the fence.

If using a standard off hand grinder, rather than the modified one in the next chapter, temporarily removing the side cover may assist in getting the rest into position. Ideally, the edge of the rest's table should only be a few millimeters from the wheel so as to limit the amount that the drill is required to project from the jig.

Set the table at 25 to 30 degrees to the wheel's side face and the fence at about 1 degree so that grinding only takes place on the front edge of the wheel, a stop screw is not required.

Place the drill in the vee support and, with the drill positioning bar (9) loosely fitted to the drill's shank, arrange the drill's cutting edges parallel with the jig's base and clamp in place. Next, adjust the drill end stop (7+8) to contact the end of the drill. With the positioning bar against the edge of the end stop base (7), **Photo 5**, fasten the bar to the drill shank, ensuring that the two halves of the assembly are parallel.

At this stage it would be advisable to loosen the drill in the vee support, then carefully holding the drill in the vee and against the end stop, and at the same time ensuring the positioning bar is against the base, once more clamp the drill in place.

You are now ready to start grinding the first face. However, as with other grinding operations, in particular the more critical ones, carrying out a few dummy runs with the wheel stopped and the drill just away from the wheel would be advisable. When confident that all is well, gradually feed the table towards the wheel and commence grinding, **Photo 6**.

I find it easier to keep the jig against the fence if I start with the drill in front of the wheel and movie it towards the center of the wheel. Continue increasing the feed until the

5 The drill positioning bar is against the drill end stop base. Repeating this position when rotating the drill 180 degrees will ensure that the angle is achieved with precision.

6 Sharpening taking place. Note that the rest has been mounted at the side of the wheel.

7 and 8 The four facet point.

first facet almost reaches the cutting edge. At this stage, continue wiping the drill back and forwards until very few sparks result at each pass.

Remove the drill from the jig and using the drill positioning bar to ensure the drill is rotated 180 degrees, replace the drill for sharpening the second facet, this time without adjusting the table's feed. Again keep wiping the drill across the wheel until sparks largely cease. The second facet is now finished.

Now set the angle of the table to the wheel to 10 degrees and grind the third and fourth facets, repeating the process. However, the process is a little more complex than that for the first two facets in that the amount removed is important and not just that both sides are the same. It is therefore necessary to take a very little off at a time, moving from side to side until the required result is achieved. The aim is to repeat the process until the chisel is changed into a point with all four facets meeting at the same spot. It is preferable to err on the side of taking too little off, leaving

the shortest of a flat on the chisel, say 0.008" maximum, rather than grinding away too much.

Photos 7 and 8 show the finished result on a 10mm drill and I would suggest that you use a drill of about this size when attempting to grind your first drill using the jig.

Do ensure that the table and the under surface of the jig's base are kept scrupulously clean as this will make it so much easier to move the jig on the rest's table. This is essential, as any extra friction in the movement will require more force to move the jig and therefore a greater likelihood of deflecting the jig on its mounting. Such a situation will make it less likely that an accurately sharpened drill will result.

As mentioned elsewhere in the book a soft paintbrush is the best way to keep the table and the base of the accessories clean. Always remember that an accessory placed on the workbench will pick up grinding particles so will require cleaning each time it is brought to the rest.

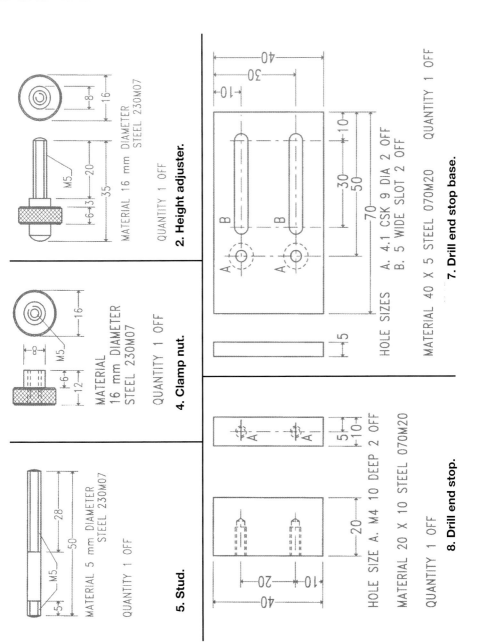

MATERIAL 5 mm DIAMETER STEEL 230M07

QUANTITY 1 OFF

5. Stud.

M5

5

28

50

MATERIAL 16 mm DIAMETER STEEL 230M07

QUANTITY 1 OFF

4. Clamp nut.

M5

8

6

12

16

MATERIAL 16 mm DIAMETER STEEL 230M07

QUANTITY 1 OFF

2. Height adjuster.

M5

6 3

35

20

8

16

HOLE SIZE A. M4 10 DEEP 2 OFF

MATERIAL 20 X 10 STEEL 070M20

QUANTITY 1 OFF

8. Drill end stop.

40

20 20

10

5

10

20

HOLE SIZES A. 4.1 CSK 9 DIA 2 OFF
B. 5 WIDE SLOT 2 OFF

MATERIAL 40 X 5 STEEL 070M20   QUANTITY 1 OFF

7. Drill end stop base.

40

30

10

B

B

A

A

10

30

50

70

5

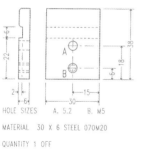

HOLE SIZES   A. 5.2   B. M5

MATERIAL 30 X 6 STEEL 070M20

QUANTITY 1 OFF

3. Drill clamp.

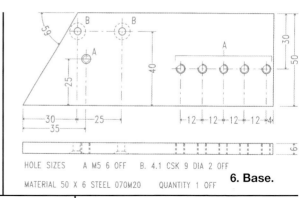

HOLE SIZES   A M5 6 OFF   B. 4.1 CSK 9 DIA 2 OFF

MATERIAL 50 X 6 STEEL 070M20   QUANTITY 1 OFF

6. Base.

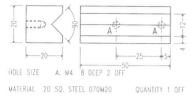

HOLE SIZE   A. M4 8 DEEP 2 OFF

MATERIAL 20 SQ. STEEL 070M20   QUANTITY 1 OFF

1. Drill support.

Even if you opt to stay with the more common drill point configuration rather than adopting the four-facet form as your standard, it would be worth making the jig in this chapter and at least experiment with the format. As the jig is so simple to make, with precision not being a requirement, there is nothing to stop you giving it a try.

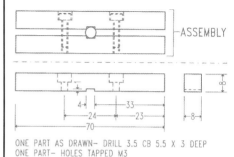

ONE PART AS DRAWN— DRILL 3.5 CB 5.5 X 3 DEEP
ONE PART— HOLES TAPPED M3

4MM GROOVE SUITS DRILLS DOWN TO 5MM DIAMETER IF REQUIRED MAKE A SECOND ASSEMBLY WITH 2MM GROVE FOR SMALLER DRILLS

USE M3 CAP SCREWS
LENGTHS TO SUIT DIAMETER OF DRILL BEING HELD

MATERIAL 8 SQ. STEEL 070M20

QUANTITY ONE OF EACH PART PER ASSEMBLY.

9. Drill positioning bar assembly.

CHAPTER 13
A TOOL AND CUTTER GRINDING HEAD

Having put to use the grinding rests seen in the previous chapters I was very pleased with the results achieved considering them to be the equal of results with more advanced equipment. However, using a standard off hand grinder, I soon became aware that having both cup and saucer wheels available would be beneficial. This is not surprising, as such wheels are standard practice for serious tool and cutter grinding. I therefore obtained a small (125mm) off hand grinder that I converted to take these.

Normal practice when using these wheels, that have larger center holes, is to fit them with permanent adapters. This enables wheels to be interchanged quickly and with only minimal need of truing up. I have included dimensioned part drawings, though these will need to be checked for your own situation. The dimensions suit a 12mm spindle and a

1 Machining the face of the added bush powered by its own motor, the spindle would be machined in a similar manner.

wheel hole size of 32mm, maybe listed as 31.75mm. Similar procedures can be used for imperial sized equipment.

On the grinder being adapted the steps in the spindle against which the wheel flanges butt was not well made and more important, only 1mm high, so was improved by the addition of the Spindle Bush (1). I did not consider this alone was adequate and machined the bush's face, while in situ, using the grinder's own motor for power. The spindle was also ½" diameter and I reduced this to 12mm to ensure it ran true and both ends were the same size. I consider that adding the bush and machining its face to be essential but reducing the spindle's diameter will depend on its initial accuracy. The following is the suggested sequence to adopt.

GRINDING MACHINE SPINDLE

Make both spindle bushes (1). Cut a piece of tube to length. Set up the grinder on the lathe bed (see later comments) and machine the

first end to 12mm diameter. While the grinder is still on the lathe, fit the first bush using two-part epoxy adhesive, holding this in place using a piece of tube and the spindle nut. Leave for a few hours. Remove the nut and tube and very lightly machine the bush's face, **Photo 1.** Remove the grinder, turn round, refit and repeat the sequence on the second end making sure that both ends are the same diameter.

MOUNTING THE GRINDER

Mounting the grinder will depend both on the type of lathe bed and the form the grinder base takes, as a result precise details cannot be given. On the plus side, only very light cuts will be taken so the security of the mounting will not be severely tested. Because of this, whatever form the bed takes, adequately mounting the grinder should not present a problem.

If concerned regarding possible damage to the slide ways some thin card packing will eliminate the possibility. Having said that the mounting will not be called upon to withstand heavy loads, do not be complacent. Do give the spindle of the grinder a good tug to check adequacy of mounting prior to machining.

When mounted, the spindle should run parallel to the lathe's axis. Using a surface gauge, with the two pins lowered and against the lathe's bed, check the position of the spindle at both ends as seen in **Photo 2**. It can be seen from this photograph that toolmaker's clamps were used to hold the grinder in place on the lathe's flat bed.

When setting up for machining the second end, allowance must be made for the different spindle diameters at that stage, ½" and 12mm in my case, use feeler gauges at one end to compensate for the difference. Absolute precision is not required as an error of as much as 0.008" will only result in a very small taper over the length of the machined spindle; aim to get both ends the same diameter next to the added bushes.

INNER AND OUTER FLANGES (2 AND 3)

The essential requirement for these is for their bore and the face that contacts the wheel and that which locates against the spindle bush to be true and parallel and the 32mm diameter concentric with the bore.

Cut four pieces of 60mm diameter, place in the three jaw and face one side of each. Then reverse, making sure that the already machined face sits cleanly on the chuck jaws, and face the second sides to 10 and 8mm thick, also bore each to a little under 12mm. It is essential that the hole in all four flanges finish up the same size.

To achieve this, continue opening up the fourth flange to 12mm diameter and leave the boring tool set at this diameter. Replace each flange in turn and open up to 12mm at one pass. Note that the outer flange is opened up to 12.5mm at a later stage.

3 Turning an end flange while mounted on a stub mandrel.

Make a 12mm Stub Mandrel using a piece of material at least 25mm diameter. Face and tap the end M8 then turn a 12mm stub 7.5mm long. The 12mm diameter must be a close fit in the flange's holes. Do not remove the mandrel from the chuck until all flanges have been machined.

Fit the first flange and machine to the 32mm and 5mm dimensions, make also the 0.5mm deep recess, **Photo 3**. Repeat for the remaining flanges. Return the two outer flanges (3) to the chuck and open up the bore to 12.5mm as per the drawing, concentricity is not crucial, as this is only the clearance for the 12mm spindle. Drill, tap and counterbore as required.

THE WHEELS

While not readily available from most suppliers to the home workshop, the wheels required are widely used in industry and

4 The two grinding wheels and the flanges for adapting the large hole in the wheels onto a smaller spindle diameter.

will therefore be available from your local abrasives supplier. The following are those that I used, though your supplier may offer something different, albeit only slightly.

- Taper cup wheel, Type 11, 125mm outer diameter, 40mm outer depth with a stated hole size of 31.75mm, grade WA60 KV1
- Saucer wheel, Type 12, 125mm outer diameter, 13mm outer depth with a stated hole size of 31.75mm, grade WA60 KV1
- Both stated a hole size of 31.75mm but both measured 32mm.

As an alternative to the taper cup (type 11) a straight-sided cup could be considered, this would be a type 6, see SK1 Chapter 1. If you adapt a 150mm grinder there is no need to increase the wheel diameters as both sizes will run at the same speed, around 2950rpm.

MOUNTING THE WHEELS

When mounting the flanges to the wheels, and these assemblies to the spindle do not over tighten the fixings. These should be tightened just sufficient to provide reliable rotation of the wheel. Over tightening must be avoided! **Photo 4** shows the two wheels, one already fitted with its flanges.

MOUNTING THE GRINDER AND REST

Both grinder and rest need to be mounted on the same rigid base, as any flexibly will cause problems with finish and accuracy, maybe also safe working. See chapter 9 SK1 for a suggested method.

To obtain maximum benefit from the wheel forms fitted on this grinder it will be necessary in some cases for the rest to be mounted at the side of the grinder. The base will need therefore to be wide enough to accommodate this requirement and at both ends, **Photo 5**. Even with a standard bench grinder with plain disk wheels this facility can be useful for some applications.

If you obtain a 125mm grinder it is likely that the rest may be a little on the high side, maybe also for a 150mm grinder. This can be overcome by using a suitable wooden packer below the grinder as photograph 5 shows.

DIRECTION OF ROTATION

I have read articles that mention the need for cutter grinder spindles to be reversing. This caused discussion on the advisability of this when using a single central nut for fixing the wheel as it may tend to come loose when

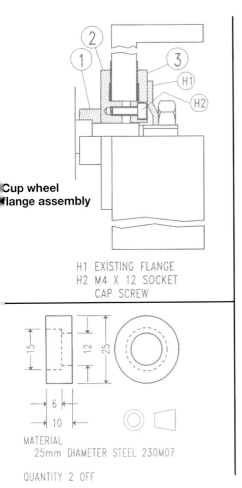

Cup wheel flange assembly

H1 EXISTING FLANGE
H2 M4 X 12 SOCKET
   CAP SCREW

MATERIAL
   25mm DIAMETER STEEL 230M07

QUANTITY 2 OFF

1. Spindle bush.

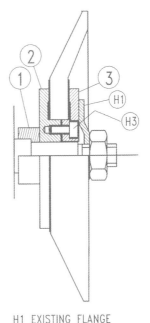

H1 EXISTING FLANGE
H3 M4 X 8 SOCKET
   CAP SCREW

Saucer wheel flange assembly

rotating in one direction. In this arrangement there will be no problem as in effect we have two spindles their direction of rotation differing from end to end. As a result the spindle has left and right hand threads to cope safely with this situation.

GUARDING

I have, chosen to retain the guards that were part of the original grinder for use with the saucer wheel, but to make an extended guard for use with the cup, again refer to Photo 5. I would suggest that, as removal and fitting of the wheels is easy, only the wheel being used should be fitted. This leaves the second

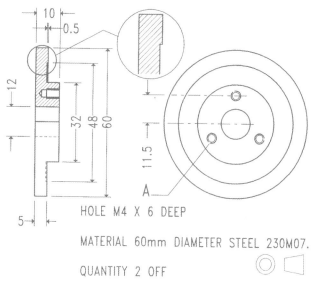

HOLE M4 X 6 DEEP

MATERIAL 60mm DIAMETER STEEL 230M07.

QUANTITY 2 OFF

2. Inner flange.

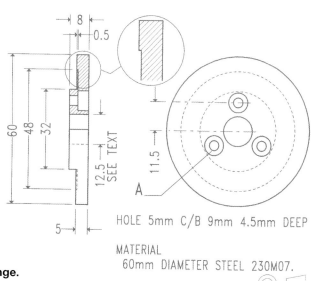

HOLE 5mm C/B 9mm 4.5mm DEEP

MATERIAL
60mm DIAMETER STEEL 230M07.

QUANTITY 2 OFF

3. Outer flange.

spindle without a grinding wheel, preventing the possibility of accidental contact.

The guard arrangement will of course depend on the design of those on the grinder as purchased and because there is likely to be variations from make to make it is impossible for me to go into precise detail. However, **SK1** and **Photos 7, 8 and 9** show my method of fitting the outer ring that permits the narrower and wider rings to be interchanged. This will enable each wheel to be fitted on either end, which may prove beneficial in a few cases.

USING THE SET UP

Actual sharpening operations will differ very little between those using a standard bench grinder and the modified one in this chapter. However, the different wheel shapes will make some tasks easier to set up. Also, particularly with the saucer wheel, a few that would be

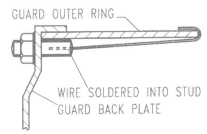

SK1. Guard assembly.

impossible with a plain wheel will become a straightforward operation. Typical of this is grinding the End Tooth Gash, this is the groove between the secondary clearance and the adjacent cutting edge, see **Photo 6**. The gash is seen being ground in **Photo 7**.

It may be thought that this is to create the cutting edge towards the center of the end mill, this is not so as the cutter only cuts

5 The rest and grinder mounted on a purpose made base. For safety, a wheel should be mounted only at the end being used.

6 View of the end of an end mill showing the end tooth gash.

at the outer end of the teeth, see Chapter 5, paragraph 2 and SK1. The purpose of the gash is to make it easier to grind the secondary clearance. It may also have some beneficial effects with swarf removal but that is beyond my level of knowledge. Even if this is the case

I would expect it only to be of real benefit at high metal removal rates.

The instructions already given in the book should also be adequate when using the grinding head in this chapter. I am though including **Photos 8** and **9** that show the grinding head being put through its paces.

A FINAL COMMENT

Having come to the end of the book I am reminded that I included in the preface a comment that stated "The ultimate success of producing accurate and correctly ground cutters depends mainly on the skill and initiative of the operator." I do hope this book has been helpful in achieving the skill and initiative required for what many would consider to be the most complex area of workshop practice.

7 Grinding the end tooth gash using a saucer wheel. This would not be possible with the disk wheels on a standard off hand grinder.

8 Set up for grinding the cutting edges of an end mill.

9 Set up for grinding the end teeth. Note this is being done with a wiping action rather than the simpler plunge and remove option that produces a less well controlled edge as it replicates errors in the wheel's face.